Swedish Lessons

Two week l

Bent

'When people say to me: "Would you rather be thought of as a funny man or a great boss?", my answer's always the same. To me they're not mutually exclusive.'

Dedicated to the memory of David Brunton, the most creative, inspirational and hilarious friend and teacher anyone could wish for.

Swedish Lessons

How Schools With More Freedom Can Deliver Better Education

Nick Cowen

Civitas: Institute for the Study of Civil Society
London
Registered Charity No. 1085494

First Published June 2008

ISBN 978-1-903386-67-5
Independence: Civitas: Institute for the Study of Civil Society is a registered educational charity (No. 1085494) and a company limited by guarantee (No. 04023541). Civitas is financed from a variety of private sources to avoid over-reliance on any single or small group of donors.

All publications are independently refereed. All the Institute's publications seek to further its objective of promoting the advancement of learning. The views expressed are those of the authors, not of the Institute.

Typeset by
Civitas

Printed in Great Britain by
The Cromwell Press
Trowbridge, Wiltshire

Contents

Author

Nick Cowen is a philosophy graduate from University College London and has been a researcher at Civitas since 2006. He has previously written *School Choice in the UK and Overseas* and co-authored a number of reports including *Ready to Read?*, an analysis of the use of synthetic phonics to teach reading in schools. He is also a volunteer teacher for the Language of Liberty Institute.

Acknowledgements

Thanks are due to Anders Hultin, Camilla Heymann and Paula Aggeval of Kunskapsskolan; Simon Varley of Internationella Engelska Skolan; Patrik Levin, Legal Officer at the Swedish National Agency for Education (Skolverket); Fredrik Bergström (director) and Nora Prochazka (research fellow), at the Swedish Retail Institute (HUI); Carl-Gustaf Stawström, CEO of the Swedish Association of Independent Schools; Mats Gerdau, parliamentary representative for Nacka, and member of the Moderate Party; and Jenny Kallstenius, department of Sociology, Stockholm University; Douglas Carswell, MP for Harwich and Clacton; and David Conway, Civitas.

Foreword

There has long been scepticism, especially on the Left, around the notion of 'school choice'. Parents and children don't want *choice*, they want a good neighbourhood school, is a common response to such proposals. This is a reasonable position. Children's education is too important for parents to have to shop around and experiment with schools by trial and error in order to find a good one. Furthermore, a good school should surely be available for every child—and choice seems to suggest an element of lottery, with the implication that there are losers. To many the 'market' element in choice sounds dangerously unregulated; a system which allows cowboys to creep in and make money by providing poor quality schools at the expense of children's learning. The introduction of competing providers also smacks of letting the government off the hook. Not everyone feels that a hands-off state is a positive; shouldn't the government therefore, rather than the market, be responsible for providing good schools?

Another fear in a system of school choice is that the less advantaged would do worse. This worry relates principally to parents' access to and utility of information, both in the sense of what makes for an effective school and in how to use the system. Related to this is a concern that this scenario would increase socio-economic segregation, as parents choose 'by class', thereby further minimising the educational opportunities of deprived children.

Many of these reservations are ones which I too have shared, both from the perspective of a policy analyst and as a teacher. Certainly, in my own experience of teaching in a primary school in Tower Hamlets, in contexts where, for example, there are many parents who speak little English, their potential to select the best school for their child within the British system would likely put them at a disadvantage compared with their English middle-class counterparts.

Furthermore, what can a Scandinavian model offer to a country as different as the UK? In many areas of social policy, particularly those relating to children, the Nordic countries are held up as exemplary. This has often led to spurious comparisons, ignoring very different taxation levels, demographic profiles and population size, not to mention cultural differences.

However, my primary reservation about school choice has been the following: why alter the structure of the system, when we *know* which elements are malfunctioning within the current schooling structure? Why not simply tackle these flaws? Is it not throwing the baby out with the bathwater to alter the system, rather than to address the malfunctions within it? It is on this point in particular that Nick Cowen's presentation of school choice wins the argument.

The most important element of Cowen's version of the Swedish school choice system is that it strives to offer, rather than sidestep, what every parent wants: a good school for their children. As Cowen argues, school choice and the pursuit of good schools are often seen to have different ends. However, it is precisely the opening up of choice in school provision that is most likely to be effective in generating good schools. School choice is *the mechanism* for generating good schools for all: in other words it is not side-stepping the end-goal parents want, but realising it.

In the current British education system, there are good schools and there are bad schools. However, on the whole, the difference between the two owes less to the teachers than to intake. The 'good' schools are disproportionately found in better-off areas, and the 'poor' schools in the less-affluent areas. Disadvantage has a huge impact on how children perform in school. From the learning support which they get at home to the food the household can afford, to the work-ethic role models that their parents provide; home-life makes a fundamental difference to how children do in school. A tight rein from Whitehall on what can be taught, how it should be taught and what outcomes should be achieved, exacerbates this home-life differentiator by thwarting teachers from pursuing the needs of their actual pupils in favour of focusing their attention on bureaucratic requirements. These back-to-front priorities, which are often accompanied by intolerable pressure from the authorities to comply with bureaucratic targets, mean that teachers are much less likely to spend long periods in 'poor' schools. The high turnover of teachers there compounds the spiral of disadvantage.

Meanwhile, in the 'good' schools the pupils are easier to teach while the parents are able to be more co-operative and therefore better able to consolidate learning at home. For this reason, research shows that the type of schooling offered by 'good' and 'bad' schools plays only a small part in the differences in achievement between pupils. For example, evidence from the Joseph Rowntree Foundation report, *Tackling Educational Disadvantage,* has found that only around 14 per cent of such differences are attributable to the quality of schooling. In other words, it is not that the teaching is necessarily better in the good schools; it is rather that the pupils are more 'teachable'; after all, the level of central dictation means that all schools are teaching the same thing, the same way.

A system of school choice, as Cowen suggests, would provide the desperately needed injection of plurality which would enable schools to respond to the needs of their pupils. Cowen's wider definition of outcomes would also be fundamental to this, in order to avoid the current situation which is based on central targets built upon the notion that 'disadvantage is not an excuse for underachievement'. Thus, within a system of school choice, the disadvantaged have a better chance to achieve than in the current system. This is true even in a scenario with a parental knowledge deficit. Cowen tackles this hurdle with his utilisation of school choice advisers, who would narrow the information gap between the haves and have-nots.

The question is, does the whole system need a shake-up in order to give schools autonomy? Yes and no. The effect of allowing diverse providers other than the government would be to bring in a diversity of pedagogies. One of the main problems in schools is a lack of diversity (allowing for responsiveness to pupils)—stemming from a lack of autonomy. Arguably, the central problem in the current education system is a lack of autonomy for teachers. The benefit of introducing a variety of providers is that they are more likely to be able to introduce alternative pedagogies. Furthermore, school choice does not represent a structural revolution. The Swedish system is entirely plausible in the UK because, although school choice may represent a revolution in outcomes, it need not represent a revolution in arrangements. The mechanisms and seeds are there. Thanks to Tony Blair's and Andrew Adonis's dabblings with pluralism (generally more in relation to funding sources than pedagogies) there are such things as 'school choice advisers'. To an extent, there is a degree of diversity, albeit limited, in the form of Academies.

This need for plurality in school provision moves into the need for plurality in accountability. Contrary to worries about a free-for-all for providers through school choice, devolving responsibility in a context regulated by Local Education Authorities as Cowen proposes, is actually the solution to the current weaknesses that have arisen through over-centralised control. With competition in this quasi-market, and pluralism in the types of provision on offer, accountability is likely to become much more meaningful than in a context where the government is sole provider.

But the most compelling reason for supporting school choice is the implication which it would have for the current private/state school chasm. The UK's two-tier education system is a great cause of concern to the Left. Many have argued that what is crippling the UK education system is the parallel independent sector. The solution is seen to be getting rid of the 'elite' schools. Paradoxically, although this is not what critics of the independent sector generally had in mind, the best way to do that is to make the private sector available to all. This is what opening up the state-funded education sector to independent providers would achieve.

To end on two caveats: firstly, education cannot be a panacea, and the impact of poverty on learning is very difficult to affect. For this reason, policy-making needs to address not only what happens in school, but also children's home lives. The second caveat is more concrete. Cowen imagines a system of school choice in which the definition of 'outcomes' is not straitjacketed—as well as definitions of effective methodologies. School choice allows a plurality of pedagogies to enter into the system as well as a comparative plurality of definitions as to what constitutes a 'good' school. Were a system of inspection, such as the current Ofsted regime, to continue within a system of school choice, this plurality would be severely constrained. Therefore the introduction of school choice would also require a reform of the inspection regime.

Anastasia de Waal
Head of Family and Education, Civitas

Executive Summary

The education gap in England

England is a middle-ranking country compared to other developed nations in terms of education outcomes. However, trends point downwards and England has a 'long tail' of reading underachievement, and a wide gap between the rich and the poor, paralleled by poor social mobility:

- **Programme for International Student Assessment (PISA):** The United Kingdom ranks 24th in maths with 495 points compared to a 498 international average. That is a 34-point decline from 2000 when our score was 529 and we were ranked 8th. In reading, the UK ranks 17th with a score of 495 compared to the international average of 492. In 2000, the UK was ranked 7th and scored 523.

- **Progress in International Literacy Study (PIRLS):** England's mean score fell from 553 in 2001, to 539, worse than Sweden, Germany, Italy, Luxembourg, even Hungary and Bulgaria. The overall mean is 539 but the 25th quartile is significantly below the international average of 500. As a consequence, England has some of the most literate children in the world; yet it also has some of the most illiterate in the developed world.

- **Department for Children, Schools and Families (DCSF):** Nearly 80 per cent of pupils eligible for free school meals are failing to achieve five GCSEs at grades A* to C, including English and maths, the government's preferred basic measure of achievement at 16.

- **The Sutton Trust:** Intergenerational mobility declined from 1958 to 1970 and from 1970 to 2000 remained at the same level.

Why the gap?

State schools are obliged to follow bureaucratic demands, both in terms of resource allocation and outcome generation. The result is more money for ring-fenced projects and national agencies, and school management required to aim for high grades rather than to provide useful knowledge and skills, producing strong incentives to lower standards in order to give the impression of greater attainment:

- In the month of January 2008 alone, the now-DCSF announced specific projects worth £727.5 million.

- In 2001 total expenditure on quangos associated with the DCSF was £8.4 billion. In 2006 it was £18.7 billion. [Economic Research Council]

- While government figures show dramatic improvements in assessment grades, research by Durham University concur with international evidence that most improvements are illusory. Instead, on average over one decade, GCSE grades have been 'inflated' by half-a-grade compared to developed pupil abilities, A-levels by one grade.

- An ICM survey in 2006 showed that 55 per cent of students felt that teachers steer them towards courses in which their school does best, rather than what they need. [Association of Colleges]

Middle-class options

With limited places at good schools under the current system, middle-class families are capable of exploiting the complexity of admissions to gain those places. When good education is scarce, middle-class families can exercise choice to supplement state provision, while the disadvantaged cannot:

- Socio-economic segregation in the school system is *worse* than segregation between neighbourhoods. [Institute for Public Policy Research (IPPR)]

- Seven per cent of British pupils attend independent schools, usually paying fees. A MORI poll suggested that half of all parents would send their children to independent schools if they could afford it. [Independent Schools Council]

- Around a quarter of all children taking GCSEs receive (often expensive) private tuition to supplement their mainstream schoolwork. [Institute of Education at the University of London]

Evidence for parent choice and more independent schools

Evidence from Sweden suggests that state-maintained schools with more independence tend to perform better and that schools perform better in areas where parents are given more choice of schools:

- In 2006, the average merit rating for pupils leaving compulsory education was 20 points higher in independent schools (225.3) than municipal schools (205.3). [National Agency for Education (Sweden)]

- In Nacka, Sweden, in 2006, where state schools are given similar levels of freedom as independent schools, average merit ratings for pupils finishing in both independent and municipal schools were the same: 231, significantly above the national average.

- Böhlmark and Lindahl (University of Stockholm) found that a ten percentage point increase in the number of independent schools produced a statistically significant increase in average grades, the majority of which was caused by improvements in surrounding municipal schools.

Free schools

UK policy should aim to:

- extend parent choice as far as possible and reduce selection as much as possible to give children equal access to good schools

- permit independent providers of education (including co-operatives, charities and companies) to open, own and manage *Free schools** and receive funding per-pupil exclusively from local authority budgets

- require Free schools to admit pupils on a first-come-first-served basis, and to comply with all relevant health and safety and child protection regulations

- make Free schools responsible for their curriculum, pedagogy, personnel and premises

- reform planning legislation so that schools can open on any site with a suitable use designation (including commercial, industrial and some residential).

Closing the gap

Sweden has also shown that more places in good non-selective schools is not sufficient to improve the education outcomes of all seriously disadvantaged children. To ensure that everyone is included reforms should:

- weight per-pupil funding so that an extra premium is given to schools that attract children eligible for free school meals

---

*   Free Schools are a direct translation of the Swedish 'Friskolor': exclusively government-funded independent schools.

- allow parents of pupils with special educational needs (SEN) statements to take direct control over their additional funds, so that they can be applied to their own choice of special educational provider

- provide a brochure (in all appropriate languages) giving details of all schools in any given area with a procedure simple enough for all families to choose a school

- ensure that free, independent advice on school choice is available to disadvantaged families.

Introduction

'If the government would make up its mind to require for every child a good education, it might save itself the trouble of providing one. It might leave to parents to obtain the education where and how they pleased, and content itself with helping to pay the school fees of the poorer classes of children, and defraying the entire school expenses of those who have no one else to pay for them.'

J.S. Mill, *On Liberty*, 1869[1]

Tucked into a housing estate in the north Stockholm district of Spånga stands a non-fee-paying but independent school. This is one of 21 secondary schools that the Kunskapsskolan ('school of knowledge') chain operates. The outside of the building is an understated redbrick, similar to the rest of the flats along the street. It is only once inside that the novelties start to leap out. No standard classrooms here, instead a number of smaller rooms for no more than a dozen pupils. They converge on a large two-storey hall that connects both levels by a series of gangways and stairs. Transparency is a key design objective: many of the interior walls and most of the doors are made of soundproof glass. Noise levels vary throughout the complex, regulated by the soundproof design, from the loud laughing in the main hall to the conversational hum in common room areas to the near silence of the seminars.

There is no one point in the day when all (or even a majority) of the pupils are in a structured classroom environment, and much of each child's day is given over to free time, some choosing to work in teams, others to work with a computer in one of the many pod-like alcoves. Even the structured lessons take the form of workshops where pupils work on their own or in small groups with a teacher helping them, rather than a traditional whole-class method. Indeed, the pupil-teacher relationship fostered in the school

1

seems informal and friendly, with only an implicit authority. This is the theory of personalised learning taken to its logical conclusion where each child has their own set of classes to attend in a given week and is allowed to get on with their work, either alone or with a group of friends. The atmosphere is almost collegiate, yet it is a school for children aged 12-16.

'You must wonder what is going on but it works!' Paula Aggeval, deputy head explains: 'Each student gets what he or she wants. If you compare it to a more a traditional class, they get to achieve so much more than what you expected them to do. Those that are rather slow and have had big problems in their other schools, when they come to us we can help them in a way that they have never been helped before. Parents are really grateful for us.'

She goes on to outline how there is rather more structure to the Kunskapsskolan method than initially meets the eye. The schools use their own teaching curriculum based around 35 steps in each subject. A child is tested when they enter the school and put on the appropriate steps. The teachers and parents then establish what they expect to see from the child in the coming term and year, how much progress they intend to make and a plan of action, including deadlines for achieving certain goals. Pupils get more latitude in how they achieve those goals, whether it is from working alone or in a group, by taking breaks in the school day or working extra hard during the day so that they have less homework. Then they check these goals as they happen.

As Aggevall says: 'We come up with a plan and check it as it happens to make sure they are achieving what they have said... I have 15 minutes each week to sit down alone with each pupil and talk about their progress and what they want to achieve. Each week we review, we get a relationship that is personal and they feel the need to work.'

The school relies on this more personal relationship between teacher and pupil to provide less coercive means for the pupil to keep up to standard. This method has proved sufficiently successful that there is a queue of parents eager to sign their children up to Kunskapsskolan schools each year and whenever this company opens a new branch in its expanding network. As Aggevall explains: 'Pupils come from many different areas and municipalities. [In some cases] they will travel for an hour to get here.'

So is personalised learning the result when you give parents the freedom to choose, and teachers the freedom to teach? Not quite—at least not necessarily.

Choice means diversity

Tucked into a commercial estate in the district of Täby, north of Stockholm, stands an independent school. This is one of eight secondary schools that the Internationella Engelska Skolan (International English School) chain operates. The outside of the building looks quite similar to the rest of the businesses along the street. Inside, the atrium leads to a large hall rather similar in style to the open architecture of the Kunskapsskolan schools. The rooms adjoining this hall, however, are of the ordinary classroom variety. Pupils sit at desks or workbenches facing the teacher, who stands in front of the whole class with a blackboard. Silence descends on the main hall during lesson times as the majority of children are occupied. The rest work quietly in a common area next to a large and well-stocked library.

The main pillar of this curriculum is a commitment to making all pupils fluent in English, as they consider it a key to making Swedes successful in the modern international economy. They achieve this by conducting more and more lessons, such as science, in English, as the children get more proficient, so that speaking and writing English becomes

3

naturally integrated into the learning environment rather than just another subject. The teaching method employed is 'performance-based learning': whole class learning combined with an emphasis on graded competitive assessment of classroom work and frequent testing in a constant drive to improve the standards of each individual pupil.

The results speak for themselves. In 2005, over 90 per cent of IES students passed with distinctions or special distinctions in English compared with the national average of 59 per cent. In 2006, the equivalent results in Swedish were 65 per cent compared to a 50 per cent national average.[2] However, in addition to following these statutory assessments that are specified by the National Agency for Education, the top students are now being encouraged to pursue qualifications in internationally recognised English-language based IGCSE examinations.

You get some idea of the pride in achievement that this school chain has by gazing along the school office wall. It is covered in diplomas, certificates, newspaper cuttings describing pupil achievements and photographs of smiling students who have just been handed awards. Elsewhere trophies gleam in cabinets. The whole atmosphere is typified by one framed slogan referenced to the Kennedy Space Center: 'Failure is not an option'. It is not just academic pursuits that are pervaded by this attitude, but also competitive sports and character building activities such as summer camps.

Embodying this 'work hard, play hard' philosophy, it is as if an elite British school has been carefully packed up, flown over the North Sea and rebuilt in a modern factory warehouse in a suburb of Stockholm; and, crucially, opened its doors to every child that chooses to go there. This is an elite school that is not only for the elite. Of course, one reason it looks this way is that a large proportion of the teaching staff, the most important resource for any school, are imported. Of around 450 members of staff throughout the entire IES chain, over 200 hail from countries other than Sweden, including Britain, Australia, Canada and the US.

The academic project manager, Simon Varley, himself a Briton, described how he has few problems attracting qualified teachers from the UK. In a three-day trip to London in November 2006, he interviewed 40 applicants, and around 80 qualified teachers from the University of Sheffield showed an interest in joining the school chain. This is despite the disadvantage that IES does not offer an equivalent level of pay as that available to teachers in the British school system. Varley can explain this apparent discrepancy: the better environment on offer for teachers. These schools do not just offer children a unique place in which to learn, but also a supportive workplace in which teachers can thrive and develop as well. Indeed, one of the new developments is the IES academy designed for their own teachers with its own curriculum based on English, pedagogy, Information Technology, bilingualism and modern philosophy.[3] Free from direct state intervention, teachers from around the world can continue to develop their skills and in a direction that they particularly appreciate rather than in a way that is statutorily required of them.

This is the main lesson of allowing the freedom to choose. What is a school *meant* to look like if you let there be choice? In fact, that is exactly what it will *not* look like: planned or predicted in advance by policy makers. Instead teachers and educationalists advance different forms of schools, and parents evaluate the results by choosing between them.

A school might look like a traditional independent school or it might use Montessori or another personalised learning pedagogy. It might use the latest technology or it might concentrate on traditional teaching methods. There might be an emphasis on science or languages, or on other activities such as sport. More than likely there will be a wide diversity catering for different families. Over time it is likely that some innovations and strategies will become more dominant, as they prove to be more successful and their best practice spreads. For example, both IES and Kunskapsskolan place significant emphasis on intervention when it comes to children at risk of being left behind in class. But exactly what those strategies will be can only be chosen by parents and by teachers once ideas have been tried out. The other great advantage of this is that improvement is open-ended. There is no termination of this discovery process at a set point when a particular school model has been enforced from above. Instead the best methods and best schools are only the best until a superior innovation comes along and spreads the better practice throughout the system.

What is school choice?

School choice rests on the assumption that the state has a major role in providing education, making it compulsory and universal, by supporting parents that cannot afford it for their children, but that total state provision of free education is potentially damaging. To prevent the state from crowding out other successful education providers, a government respects the wishes of parents and guardians by funding any school which fulfils certain pre-conditions, according to the number of pupils that attend.

Essentially, different responsibilities are delegated to those in a better position to uphold them. The government has the responsibility to fund schools; teachers and educationalists are responsible for managing schools; and parents are required to choose between the available schools. So long as the system is permitted to be responsive to the choice that parents make, no child need go without a place at a desired school. This way schools and teachers can be given a large degree of autonomy while continuing to receive government funding.

Support for school choice in some form has been around since the state first became involved in education provision. There are essentially two arguments for it. The first is the case for diversity and the view that universal compulsory state education is a threat to personal autonomy. As John Stuart Mill argued nearly 150 years ago:

> A general State education is a mere contrivance for moulding people to be exactly like one another: and as the mould in which it casts them is that which pleases the predominant power in the government, whether this be a monarch, a priesthood, an aristocracy, or the majority of the existing generation, in proportion as it is efficient and successful, it establishes a despotism over the mind, leading by natural tendency to one over the body.[4]

So, by allowing parents to decide (within limits) what sort of education is suitable for their children, it can be ensured that there will always be some diversity of pedagogy and curriculum within any nation state. In a society of competing ideas, the power of government to control what people learn is naturally limited—a pre-requisite for maintaining a community based on liberty.

The second argument is that school choice tends to generate better educational outcomes due to increased teacher autonomy and incentives to focus on what parents want rather than what the state requires. Whatever model one proposes, it cannot be known *a priori* that independent teachers and parents with a choice tend to produce a better education for children than a system controlled by the state. However, on this front, there is a growing body of empirical evidence that both private schools and government funded independent schools generally have better outcomes than their state-managed counterparts in developed countries. As a recent Sutton Trust report has found:

> ... private schools tended to be ahead, notably in Germany, Canada, Ireland, the Slovak Republic and the Netherlands, even after adjustments for background. Macao-China, Spain, Korea and Thailand have both independent and government-dependent private schools and there was a progression in the PISA 2003 maths scores from the fully independent doing best to the government schools doing worse.[5]

Swedish surprise

In a quirk of history, the most radical form of state-funded but independently managed schools has not been enacted in the UK, where fee-paying independent schools remain popular amongst a sizeable minority. Instead it has taken place in Sweden, a country that, before the reform, had an education sector of which independent schools comprised less than one per cent.

Sweden's school choice reform is unique in that it is systematic: offering the same right to choose to every family in every area, regardless of background, and in all years of schooling from primary to post-16 education. However, while offering parents a previously unprecedented level of choice, they also took steps to make sure that the new system was compatible with Sweden's egalitarian values by banishing pupil selection from independent schools entirely. Despite being systematic, the reform did not involve opening any new schools or shutting down any state schools but merely changing the rules under which new schools could be allowed to open. In other words, this was not a revolutionary or destructive reform but one in which newly established schools were neatly integrated into the system of state schools with a minimum of disruption.

As a consequence, despite the significant differences in the way Sweden was and the way the United Kingdom is today, there are a number of lessons we can take from the reform. The most important is that a robust policy of school choice does not have to compromise on the principle of equality of opportunity for all, so long as correct measures are taken to include everyone. While more conservative theories of school choice demand a minimum level of provision for every child, Sweden's model goes further: a system that aims to use school choice *as a means* to offer an equal level of provision for every child.

For better or worse, the education policy debate in the UK has tended to focus on measurable outcomes with underlying economic benefits, rather than on education for the sake of knowledge itself. As a consequence, this report also focuses on the policy debate as it stands at the moment, about what school choice can do for those practical outcomes. This should not be taken as an endorsement of this limited view of education, merely an acceptance that it is the debate over this narrower question of outcomes that must be resolved before asking the wider questions of what education is really for.

The purpose of this report is to examine critically school choice in Sweden, both its benefits and problems, and analyse how we can apply lessons learnt in Sweden to the context of the education system in England. Chapter one combines an overview of the Swedish school system with evidence based on interviews with several experts who approach the system from different perspectives. Chapter two considers the implications this evidence has for schools in England and discusses the debate surrounding education. Chapter three sets out some specific policy recommendations for bringing about school choice.

1

School Choice in Sweden

In 1992 the Swedish government made a simple systematic decentralising reform of the education system. Up until then, practically every school was publicly owned and publicly managed. Beyond a few isolated experiments, a few privately managed schools with special permission to receive government funding, the small number of private schools (90 in 1992)[1] were fee paying and unavailable to the majority of Swedish families. Essentially, Swedish local authorities (known as municipalities) were the sole providers of education. The only change in recent years had been to give these local municipalities full financial control over the schools in their district.

The reformed policy offers a general right for any individual or organisation to apply to open a school for children in the compulsory age-range (7-16 in Sweden)[2] and 'upper-secondary' age-range (16-18).[3] If the school plan fulfils the requirements set out under the reform according to the Swedish National Agency for Education (or Skolverket), it receives funding for each pupil (often called vouchers) out of the municipal school budget. In other words, this allows anyone who fits certain universal criteria to offer an education to pupils on equal footing with state provision.

The second part of this reform focuses on the parents: rather than there being any banding, or selection by schools or municipal officials, families decide which school to send their children to and are permitted to send their child to any school with any spare capacity. The right to choose does not apply just for selecting independent schools, but also to any municipal school with spare capacity. In other words, it is not just a choice between a local school and a private school but a choice of any school in the entire system. Though pupils are still assigned a local school by default, the aim of this reform was that *no one* should be compelled to use a government school if they thought it was inadequate or underachieving.

Despite this relative freedom, independent schools, or 'friskolor' ('Free schools'), exist under several financial and pupil-entrance conditions. They must first be approved for state voucher funding by Skolverket and can only accept fees through per-pupil state funding. They are not allowed to ask for 'top-up' fees from parents. Compulsory schools are not allowed, in the case of over-subscription of available places, to select pupils on any basis other than the order in which they applied to join the school (an exception is allowed for siblings of children already at the school who are allowed priority). Upper secondary schools (post-16) have slightly more leeway, and can set basic standards (assessed by national examinations) for pupils' eligibility to enter a course. But they are not allowed to 'skim' the best pupils from any given group that wants to enter and must still accept pupils that have been established as eligible in the order in which they apply.

Funding

Funding arrangements have varied since the reform was introduced but they have always been exclusively based on a voucher attached to each pupil. Independent schools began by receiving 85 per cent of the funding provided per pupil in the municipal school system. This reflected part of the reasoning behind the reform (an attempt to make the education system more cost-effective) but mainly, as Bergström and Blank explain, 'to avoid putting the municipal schools at a disadvantage, since the municipalities would still have to account for various administrative and overhead costs related to their overall responsibility for the school system'.[4] Municipalities have to guarantee a place at a local state school if a family wants one, whereas independent schools merely have to register their maximum capacity.

Initially, independent schools were allowed to charge some fees but this was abolished in 1997.[5] Per-head expenditure on independent school pupils was lowered to 75 per cent of municipal school pupil funding in 1995, but then increased to 100 per cent in 1997. By 2001, the system seemed to settle on parity with municipal schools.[6] As a consequence there is some limited variation between the amount of funding pupils attract since municipalities have slightly different per-pupil spending regimes in their own municipal schools (see section 'constraints on parents'). In addition, if a municipality has a policy of spending more on a pupil with special needs, that extra funding is also carried with the pupil to the independent school's budget if the parents choose to send their child there.

There remain a few minor controversies on funding, however. Carl-Gustaf Stawström, CEO of the Swedish Association of Independent Schools, says that several municipalities continue to try to deduct a small administration fee from the premium that each pupil takes with them to an independent school, in contravention of the way the law is currently framed: '[There are] small schools who know that the municipality does not give the same money, because they charge the independent schools for the legal responsibility of keeping some places open in [municipal] schools. They have no legal coverage for that, but they take those decisions and you have to go to court to get it back.'

Upper secondary voluntary schools have a slightly different funding arrangement. Pupils opt for one of 17 national programmes (ranging from natural sciences through electrical engineering to media).[7] The content of the programmes varies from school to school and there are several subjects within each programme, but municipalities are required to make each programme available in some form to every pupil in their district. If an independent school offers a programme, then the premium that a pupil attracts is equivalent to what they would have cost if they had accepted the programme at a local municipal upper secondary school. If there are no municipal schools offering that particular programme in the pupil's home district, then the cost is decided by a national price list for the 17 programmes. Vocational courses (such as media studies) often attract rather more per-pupil funding than academic courses due to the increased cost of equipment and supervision.

Since local municipalities have some freedom in setting the value of the voucher for each year group, it is difficult to generalise over what 'ordinary' per-pupil funding is but it tends to vary between 40,000 and 70,000 Swedish Kronor (SEK) for each pupil per annum over the various year groups. For example, Nacka, one Stockholm municipality, provides SEK 41,700 for primary pupils, SEK 47,200 for pupils aged 10-13 and SEK 60,800 for pupils ages 13-16. Upper-secondary school programmes in Nacka have an average spend of SEK 68,500 per annum for each pupil.[8]

A recent economic study measured the mean for all compulsory school pupils at SEK 54,720.[9] On exchange that is equivalent to around £4,340 but in terms of local purchasing power, according to the OECD,[10] that is equivalent to only around £3,780.

By way of an overall system comparison, the OECD estimates total expenditure per pupil at all levels of the Swedish system to be equivalent to around $7,500 for primary school pupils and $8,000 for secondary pupils (adjusted for purchasing power parity) compared to the

UK's approximately $6,000 for primary and $7,000 for secondary (PPP adjusted).[11]

It is significant that the independent school sector grew rapidly from the beginning despite *no* starting capital grants being provided by local or national government. Independent schools had to finance their starting costs. As a consequence, few independent schools have premises that have been built specifically for them and many do not own their buildings. According to Stawström: 'a clear majority of independent schools rent property, in many cases on "the free market" (converted office property) but also as rent from the municipality (school buildings)'. As it has turned out, the promise of a predictable long-term income via pupil vouchers is more valuable for establishing a new school than receiving large capital grants up-front.

Extent

Since the reform has been enacted, the number of independent schools has expanded rapidly, from 90 compulsory schools in 1992 to 585 in 2005, representing nearly 12 per cent of the total number of compulsory schools and teaching 74,000 pupils (7.44 per cent of all pupils). The number of independent upper secondary schools has risen from 57 to 266, representing 33 per cent of the total number of upper secondary schools, teaching 47,256 pupils (13 per cent of students aged 16-18).[12]

Michael Sandström, in a report for the Adam Smith Institute, notes that part of the reason for the phenomenal rise is due to allowing for-profit companies to establish schools: 'Since larger [for-profit] companies running several schools are allowed, the expansion of independent schools has been more rapid than it otherwise would have been... while successful non-profit schools have no incentive to expand, for-profit schools do. In Sweden, where both for-profit and non-profit schools exist, [for profit] schools have expanded rapidly and established subsidiary schools, the non-profit schools instead tend to create waiting lists.'[13] Around half of independent schools are run by limited companies, although few in actuality make enough money to pass on any profits to shareholders.[14] This highlights how the motivation for opening a school, even as a limited company, is generally more pedagogical than profitable.

Despite rapid expansion, independent schools remain very much in the minority. Bergström has noted that the highest levels of growth in the independent sector were experienced in the first two years of the reform, at 58.6 per cent in 1993 and 26.2 per cent in 1994, levelling down to 6.8 per cent in 2004. He suggests: 'A possible explanation for this may be that independent schools are not allowed to charge any school fees and hence the incentives for starting up new schools may decrease.'[15]

On the other hand, in terms of numbers (as opposed to percentage growth) of independent schools, there are more than ever before. In response, the number of municipal schools decreased by 252 by 2004.[16] Skolverket received around 600 applications to open new independent schools in 2007, an all time high.

Diversity

The expansion of independent schools has brought some greater diversity into the sector, although the largest category of school profiles are those that are pitched towards the mainstream:

- 38 per cent general profile—mainstream school

- 33 per cent special pedagogy (e.g. Montessori or Steiner)

- 13 per cent confessional—(e.g. Jewish or Protestant)

- five per cent language or ethnic focused (e.g. International English School)

- five per cent special profile (e.g. music or sports specialist)

- six per cent 'other'[17]

It appears that allowing new schools of various types to open has not led to a significant proliferation of agendas, ideologies or religious views in the sector, or as Mats Gerdau of the Moderate Party puts it, 'we don't have that many "weird" schools'. The diversity of school types is, instead, focused on the different pedagogies and curriculum profiles on offer.

There are a few common forms of independent school. One group comprises independent schools with a general profile that frequently form in sparsely populated rural areas when a municipal school is threatened with closure due to supposed lack of demand. This reflects a similar problem in the UK where there are currently over 100 state-funded village schools planned for closure.[18] Instead of closing, forcing children to be educated further away from home, in Sweden these premises are sometimes taken over by independent schools, often established by local parents.[19] This partly explains why independent schools are, on average, significantly smaller than municipal schools: they can continue to operate as local schools even after municipalities have decided they would be uneconomic to keep open.

Other popular schools are often part of large for-profit chains such as Kunskapsskolan, Pysslingen[20] and Vittra.[21] Bergström, director of the Swedish Retail Institute, is not surprised by this tendency towards the mainstream, seeing a parallel between providing 'normal' education and the behaviour of providers in other sectors: 'Where is the money? The money is where the many are. Most schools are normal schools but try to differentiate a little bit. [For example] look at clothing or shoes, most shops focus on the normal customer but try to differentiate themselves.'

As a consequence, differentiation and focusing on special programmes is not the preserve of explicitly specialist, nor even independent, schools as more municipal (particularly upper secondary) schools are now choosing to augment their general profile. As Stawström explains: 'five per cent have a special profile, but it doesn't mean that these 38 per cent [with a general profile] give exactly the same thing as the other schools. All these schools have programmes with a special profile and today even the public schools give special profiles as well. You don't have to choose an independent school to get a special profile.'

It should be noted that although there is a sizeable minority of schools with a particular religious profile, they are not given any special permission to select pupils on the basis of their beliefs or practices, as is currently allowed with faith schools in the UK.

The best of both worlds?

It would be easy for free market ideologues to get carried away and assume that Sweden has endorsed complete deregulation of education. However, this is simply not the case. The policy is designed specifically to allow new schools into the state sector while not causing significant disruption to the already existing schools. At the same time, the need for equality of provision is put at the heart of the system. In other words, the system is designed to deliver the flexibility of a market along with the guaranteed standards and equity of state provision.

Patrik Levin, a legal officer at Skolverket, warns about how easy it is for some policy makers to get carried away with rhetoric: 'we get all these calls from municipalities run by liberal politicians. They think it is a free market. They want to transform all municipal schools into independent schools. But we tell them, according to this [education] act, it isn't!' He is emphatic that 'according to the national act... a compulsory school has a right to grants *if it is approved by us*'.

School regulation

This system of application and approval is designed to ensure that every school available to parents matches some fairly rigorous standards and that they do not pose a threat to the existing school system. It takes place in two steps: the first to evaluate the suitability of the proposal for a school; the second to establish what the likely effects that the school will have on municipal schools in the area.

Step one involves going into some detail about the proposed independent school: describing what sort of profile the school will have and its capacity (a minimum of 20 students). Applicants have to demonstrate, often with market research, that there is evidence for demand for a school of that size and type in the area.

They must also demonstrate how they will get suitable premises for the school, how they will get qualified teachers and how they can deliver a service 'equal to the education the children would get in a public school'[22] while still remaining financially viable. Applicants must also follow the national curriculum,[23] although it should be noted that Sweden's compulsory national curriculum differs from the UK in the crucial respect that it is 'goal-based' rather than prescriptive of particular teaching methods. In other words, Skolverket sets the objectives (what pupils should know by a certain stage) but does not set out stipulations on how they should be achieved as is the case in the UK.

Nevertheless, Skolverket does issue significant guidance for timetabling compulsory school lessons and many of these goals will define much of the required content of the lessons. Schools must also agree to safeguard Sweden's 'fundamental values' including a commitment to democracy and human rights,[24] and demonstrate how they will do so. It is worth noting that while independent schools must demonstrate a robust policy on employing suitable teaching staff, they are not restricted to only employing those that have a degree in education at the government-run teaching colleges. They can make alternative arrangements, though many independent schools choose not to. The reason for this is that even schools that train their teachers in their own pedagogy still appreciate their teachers having a broad knowledge of education theory and practice, which the Swedish teacher training programme is generally considered to provide.

Proposed schools also have to explain how the school admissions policy is compatible with providing fair access to everyone with a right to attend the sort of school being proposed. For most mainstream compulsory schools this means that they will not admit students other than on the basis of the order in which their families apply.

How do independent school managers find this stage of the application? Carl-Gustaf Stawström, CEO of the Swedish Association of Independent Schools, believes that Skolverket are 'basically fair' in their decisions:

> I think, to be honest, a lot of the applications that are turned down, are turned down because the people behind the application are not clever enough to fill in the forms! I don't have figures together but I think it is the rather less serious applicants that are turned down... If they are serious people making an application and apply to start something which gives the students more choice then they often grant the applications: a serious offer that will give a bigger 'table' of choices.

To pass step two, the proposed school cannot have too great a negative effect on the public schools in the area. Taking many pupils from a local municipality would drain the public schools in the area of funds, forcing them to lose staff and eventually shut down. Some disruption is expected (and permitted) whenever a new school opens but if the local school system is likely to be reeling from the competition four or five years after the new school has been opened, then the school will be turned down for municipal grants. As Levin explains: 'If the effects are too negative, we say the basic conditions are met but that it would cause these two municipal schools to close, which may reduce choice... Everyone has a right to a local municipal school.'

It is in this area where municipalities have a 'right to reply' and add their response to the application process. Levin: 'They come back with different comments, such as "this is fine, we are positive about this school", or "this is not good" and they try and demonstrate with facts and figures how it will be negative.' Independent schools that already exist in the district are not consulted on the approval of new independent schools and receive no special protection at all in Skolverket's calculations: they are expected to compete more freely with any newcomers. Beyond giving their recommendations, municipalities have no capability to hold back an application from being approved if Skolverket consider the negative effects on other schools to be insignificant.

The time this whole process takes is significant. Applications for new schools are submitted each April but are not approved until around October and December that year (much of that time spent on getting and considering the view of the local municipality). At that point, failed applicants have an option to appeal to a court, although successful appeals are rare. This means that the soonest any approved schools can open is the following September. So the entire process takes at least 18 months.

Skolverket's regulation of independent schools does not end with this application, although their powers to intervene forcefully are more limited once a school is open. The school is approved on the basis of the profile, capacity and the curriculum it has set out in the initial application and is not allowed to deviate from this design without re-applying for permission. As Levin says: 'If they do other than what they said, they have to explain themselves. If they want to change the programme, they must also get further approval.'

It is through this application process that the Swedish government keeps a tight rein on the independent school sector, and the fact that part of the process is explicitly designed to protect already existing schools brings into question how much this system could be described as a competitive market. On the other hand, it is possible to see this policy of offering some protection to municipal education authorities as a quid pro quo required to prevent dramatic market failures: independent schools have no protection but nor do they have any legal responsibility to the sector as a whole. As Carl-Gustaf Stawström of the Swedish Association of Independent Schools explains, 'in our association, we would say let the market decide. But it is a little more difficult when talking about children. You can end up with 70 or 80 students without school places.'

Purer competition between all schools, it is argued, would occasionally open up large school-sized gaps in provision. It would then be a race against time to fill that gap as children cannot be allowed to go without education for long. Patrik Levin explains the municipalities' difficulty: 'The big thing is the occasional bankruptcy. Then it is the municipality that has to take responsibility. They can incur a lot of extra costs from a school that suddenly goes bankrupt.'

So the problem that Skolverket's regulation attempts to ameliorate is the mismatch between the responsibilities of the municipalities and independent schools. Independent schools are only responsible for their actual pupils. Municipalities, by contrast, *have* to provide a local municipal school place to every child who wants one. They also have to be prepared to step in whenever an independent school shuts down, or fails to open as expected. In other words, they have the responsibility of potential pupils to consider as well as those currently in their municipal schools. The extra protection from competition provided to municipal schools is an attempt to balance this responsibility.

This particular form of regulation might not be the best way of avoiding gaps in school provision, however. An 18-month waiting period for a new school opening, which this regulation entails, is likely to significantly slow down a potential competitive response to a bankrupt school, threatening to put even more pressure on a municipality than is already entailed by such an extreme situation. Although Bergström thinks that in practice large-scale failures will continue to be rare, he also maintains that there still needs to be an alternative model to allow municipalities to fulfil their responsibilities: 'a risk premium' deducted from the independent school voucher that municipalities retain as a form of insurance policy for pupils. This would entail a return to a proportionately lower level of funding for independent schools, though perhaps not as low as the 85 per cent used in the initial 1992 school choice reform.

Constraints on parents

The Swedish voucher system prevents education providers from competing on one measure present in more ordinary sectors: price. The cost of the voucher is set by the amount given to municipal schools for each pupil. The municipalities make the final decision on the value, indeed they (rather than parents) are permitted to top-up investment in education using local taxation. But the value of the voucher is heavily influenced by the block grants given by the national government to the municipalities. Parents have no direct control over what the value of the voucher attached to their child is, nor are they allowed to top it up from their own funds. In addition, schools must accept the value of the voucher, despite the variation across districts.

This, very occasionally, turns out to be a problem in upper secondary schools, where pupils are more likely to be travelling to school from other districts and individual course programmes have their own prices. This means that some schools can be susceptible to price fluctuations that have very little to do with the quality of education they are offering, or the demand for it. For example, a municipality may decide to cut the budget of its 'in-house' media programme to concentrate finances elsewhere, in a way that seems sensible in that local district. But any students attending a media programme at a school in another district will have their voucher funding reduced as well in parity with the reduction at the local municipal schools.

Overall, the variation between vouchers across districts is limited and does not change all that much from year to year, but when it does, it bears little relation to decisions taken by families or independent schools. This means that a significant element of the incentive structure in an ordinary market system is missing. 'I see it as an inefficiency', explains Bergström, 'If fees were allowed, the fees could function as a signal of the quality. If a school is better, you are prepared to pay a bit more. But it is politically impossible... In Sweden, you have high taxes [and] the median Swedish family does not have any net assets whatsoever.'

The purpose of these rules is to reinforce equality of access to all schools. If fees were permitted, rich parents could afford to spend their way into getting their children a better education. There is also the argument that schools might use price, not as a method of regulating their costs in providing education, but to control who can gain access to the school so that they have a learning environment that is easier to manage and profit from, creating an intentionally segregated system that benefits the advantaged more than the disadvantaged.

Models of school choice

Behind these policies that regulate price and quality lies a wider debate in Sweden about what the preferred concept of 'school choice' is. As one National Agency for Education study explains: 'The expression of school choice has been used with different meanings at different times' and while 'both the social democrats and the moderates view school choice favourably [their] views diverge when it comes to interpretation and application. The moderates consider it desirable that all schools be transformed to "independent" and "free" schools while the social democrats... maintain that there must be a balance between local authority and independent schools if one is to be able to talk about school choice at all.'[25]

So while there is mainstream consensus that the current system of school choice is generally good, why that is so and where it should be going in the future are still disputed. The debate is perhaps best described as involving two competing models of school choice. One model, broadly endorsed by the Social Democratic party, sees 'real school choice' as being between state schools and independent schools. The choice to go to an independent school is justified because it is popular with parents. Choice and diversity themselves are

24

valued as perhaps a 'bonus' in an already well-functioning system that does not require significant overhaul.

General Social Democrat Party policy as a consequence is to aim conservatively 'for a balance between the two types of school while retaining the neighbourhood principle' (the right to attend a local state school).[26] The constraining policies, under this model, are actively designed to prevent a competitive market developing rather than simply protecting pupils from market failures. In essence, this view is suspicious of what sort of educational provision independent schools would produce and holds that state intervention will always be necessary to create desired outcomes.

The alternative model, closer to the view of the Moderate party, considers direct state provision without giving ultimate choice to parents to be a barrier to innovation, improvement and efficiency in the education sector. The answer is to reduce the distinction between independent and municipal schools. This model sees 'school choice' as not so much an end, but a powerful means by which to generate better educational outcomes. Their general direction of policy is to introduce 'a completely free choice of school combined with a national capitation allowance without any neighbourhood principle'. Accordingly, the voucher would remain capped but the arbitrary differences in values between municipalities, as well as the assumption that a local state school is the first choice for parents, would be removed. In 2007, the Moderates gained a majority coalition in the Swedish Parliament, suggesting that this direction of policy may become a reality over the next few years.

Outcomes

Despite ambiguities over how competitive this system of school choice is in theory, in practice school choice has shown a number of successes on several fronts. Comparing the basic results between municipal and independent schools is itself revealing:

- In 2006, the average merit rating for pupils leaving compulsory education (age 16) was 20 points higher in independent schools than municipal schools (225.3 compared to 205.3). Amongst pupils leaving independent schools, 93.5 per cent were eligible to attend an upper secondary school, compared with 89.2 per cent from municipal schools.[27] Results at the upper secondary school level were also encouraging. Average grade points at independent schools were 14.5 (out of 20) compared to the 14.1 national average.[28]

- In addition, a study conducted by the National Agency for Education suggests that school choice now commands a high level of support amongst families. Parents tend to be more satisfied when they make a choice of school, especially if they choose an independent school: 'favourable assessments apply in particular to those who chose independent schools'. In contrast: 'There is… a small proportion of parents who state that they are not happy with the schools. These are mainly those who did not choose a school.'[29]

These results are important considering the strict entrance regulations that formally give families equal right to access the independent sector. At the same time, we cannot take them at face value, as the self-selection of families to attend independent schools, as well as geographical variations in independent school coverage, will influence results. In addition, independent schools teach a small proportion of pupils in the whole Swedish school sector. So what is more important than these figures is the effect that greater choice is having on the system as a whole. In other words, is competition driving up standards? Here too, there is a strong and growing background of evidence to suggest improvements.

Sandström and Bergström, using extensive data of 28,000 compulsory school leavers in 1997/1998 (only five years after the initial reform), found in 2002 that the 'extent of competition from independent schools, measured as the proportion of students in the municipality that goes to independent schools, improves both the test results and the grades in public [i.e. municipal] schools... The improvement is significant both in statistical and real terms. This result holds for test results, final grades and for the likelihood that a student will leave school with no failing grades.'[30]

The same study also found that the 'results give no support to the hypothesis that independent schools are more likely to be established in municipalities with "easy customers", i.e. few low-ability students.' This seems to suggest that it is indeed the effect of competition that is driving up standards and that this effect is not limited to already advantaged pupils.[31]

Åsa Ahlin, an economist at Uppsala University, used a random sample of 8,500 pupils from the same 1997/1998-year of national tests. This separate, smaller but more detailed, study did not demonstrate quite the same level of confidence in choice in some areas as Sandström and Bergström have, finding little evidence of improvement in language scores.[32] However, that same study managed to quantify much more significant beneficial effects of competition on mathematics test scores: 'A ten per cent increase in the local share of private school enrolment has a statistically significant positive effect on student performance in mathematics, corresponding to approximately one fifth (0.17) of a standard deviation in math performance. This effect is of the same magnitude as a ten percentile increase in sixth grade math test scores.'[33]

Interestingly, this benefit was felt especially amongst immigrant groups:

[I]n the case of immigrant students born outside the EU and the Nordic countries, the interaction term for school competition is statistically significant on a five per cent level with respect to mathematics. That is, the gain from increased school competition is significantly higher for this group of students than for others. For example, a ten per cent increase in the degree of school competition corresponds to a further nine percentile improvement in math test scores—almost twice the average impact. [34]

For this group, these more significant test improvements applied not only to mathematics but Swedish too: 'Immigrant students do also seem to gain from increased school competition with respect to the probability of obtaining a higher grade in the Swedish test. This effect is about ten times as large as the average impact of an increased private school share on Swedish performance, but statistically significant at a ten per cent level only.'[35]

There were also disproportionately greater improvements in mathematics for students with special needs: 'Students having attended special educational classes during the seventh or eighth grade gain more than others from increased competition in terms of mathematics performance. This gain corresponds to a five percentile improvement in the test score distribution relative to other students when the share of private school students increases by ten percentage points. This result is statistically significant on a five per cent level.'[36] Ahlin's study, therefore, seems to concur with Sandström's and Bergström's view but also suggests that the system tends to have different effects on specific sections of society.

A more recent study by economists at Stockholm University, Anders Böhlmark and Mikael Lindahl, used a broader dataset of around 20 per cent of graduating students from 1988 to 2003. Their results seem to show with more confidence, and with some quantification, what previous studies have indicated: 'the effect on average grades of a ten percentage point increase in the private school share is just below one percentile rank point. This effect is statistically significant, very stable across specifications and does not seem to be driven by differential grade-setting standards [or grade inflation] in private and public schools.'[37]

The authors note that competition between schools appears to be by far the biggest factor in this improvement: 'The individual gain from attending a private school (the private-attendance effect) is estimated to be only a small part of the total effect, about 0.1 percentile rank point. Thus, the total achievement effect is mainly driven by other people's choice of private school in the municipality. We interpret this as evidence of competition effects where more school competition forces all schools to improve.'[38] In other words, while individual students certainly receive, on average, a boost from attending an independent school, the more significant effects are in the schools in the surrounding district improving their standards.

This study also finds that 'no group is found to lose from a higher private school share',[39] although they concur with Ahlin that some groups might, at least initially, be receiving a disproportionate benefit from the system: 'Children of parents with long [higher] education and/or immigrant background are more likely to be sorted into private schools, when the private school share increases.'[40]

Segregation

The main anxiety over school choice is its potentially segregating impact: the division of pupils by schools along socio-economic background, academic levels or ethnic lines. Despite the equal and open admission rules that independent schools have, there is some evidence that this is taking place. Indeed it is implied by Böhlmark and Lindahl's evidence that there is some 'sorting' of pupils in independent schools and that their benefits are not spread evenly over the whole of Swedish society.

Although their evidence suggests no group's performance is impaired by the growth of independent schools, some families appear to be left out and do not receive a specific benefit from the new system. In addition to the question of how better outcomes in education are distributed under a situation with more school choice, a much larger question is one of social cohesion. Is a system based purely around pupil performance a *good* one?

'To speak only about performance and ability is to make it too simple', explains Jenny Kallstenius, a sociologist at the University of Stockholm, who has examined the school choices of 70,000 Stockholm pupils for an in-progress doctoral thesis. Her evidence is also based on a year of fieldwork in which she followed six different classes in two inner-city Stockholm schools. She has found that around 20 per cent of the pupils she studied went to an actively chosen school (rather than going to their local municipal school). Her findings demonstrate a trend for children in suburbs of Stockholm not so much to attend a local independent school over their local municipal school, but instead to travel to a more successful municipal or independent school in the city centre. At least initially, these pupils have several specific features. They include pupils with highly educated parents and families with the 'strongest connection to the labour market' (families which spend the least time unemployed).

There are also more choices being made from some low employment, ethnically segregated suburbs, but they tend to be made by families of immigrant backgrounds who (even if they have a poor employment record in Sweden) would have been in the more educated workforce in their countries of origin. In other words, a key, and unsurprising, feature of these families (regardless of ethnic background) is that they already consider education to be valuable. At the same time, while these are certainly the first groups of people to take advantage of school choice, they are not the only ones, as school choice becomes more common. Kallstenius finds that news tends to spread within ethnic communities, and so one satisfied parent from one community may draw others from the same community (even if they are not necessarily as highly educated).

Bergström sees this uneven growth in access, with the educated taking advantage first, followed more hesitantly by others, as a symptom of the fact that the system has only recently been opened up: 'If you typically look at recently deregulated markets, people don't know what the important factors are. They don't want to make decisions. But people eventually get more savvy about it.'

In terms of the impact on segregation, Kallstenius makes a distinction between the impact on the individual family and the rest of the community:

> If you look at specific individuals, [school choice] is a way of dealing with segregation. If you live in a particular suburb, then this system is a way to find 'keys', opening the door to the rest of society by going to a high status mainstream school. For these individuals, it is possible to get a better future career but also to learn the 'codes' of the rest of society. If you learn how most people think you should behave, you can adopt that behaviour. Including language, accents, how you dress, values and taste... Many young people and parents believe that if they go to an inner city free [independent] school, they will get this. And not get it in a suburban school.

In other words, for an immigrant family with high educational and social aspirations, school choice offers an additional opportunity for their children to succeed and integrate. The problem, according to Kallstenius, is what the choices of these families lead to on a group level: 'on a school level, segregation is becoming deeper and more widespread. The socio-economic differences are now greater between schools. The differences have become bigger when we look at different schools.'

As a consequence, Kallstenius has found that the difference in grades, between schools that receive pupils from further away and those that are losing pupils from their local areas, is also increasing: 'The differences in grades is growing, between suburban and inner-city schools... most of the students with good performance leave and go to schools in other areas. Some schools are drained.'

This 'brain drain' is not just creating inequality on the school level, but also reducing the educational advantages to those left behind who do not have the more successful pupils to learn from and look up to in their classes. Kallstenius is not certain whether this 'peer effect' is greater or lesser than the benefits these same pupils receive through schools driving up teaching standards to compete for pupils. There are some other factors that may be worsening average performance of some schools than this drain of particular sorts of pupils: 'there is a large inflow of immigrant students so they constantly struggle to keep up language standards. Refugees may have particular problems and municipal schools receive these individuals first by default.'

Nonetheless, she has seen that peer groups are a major factor even as competition takes place: 'many people talk about the "peer effect", that if you are in a classroom good pupils will encourage the rest of the pupils. Whether the peer effect is bigger than the competition is a matter of debate. But I see the peer effect in my fieldwork, with my own eyes, and listen to pupils, and from this I see the peer effect is very important. But the competition effect takes place too, as the municipal schools have to work harder to retain their pupils.'

Together with this sort of segregation, where the successful pupils within an ethnic group leave to go to more mixed schools in different neighbourhoods, Kallstenius also believes that something akin to 'white flight' is taking place amongst some Swedes: 'In other independent schools, it does tend to be ethnic Swedes that want to go to a homogenous school. They feel threatened by new accents and languages.'

Despite the additional choices available to families, the fact that only a few families take full advantage of the system and others are using it deliberately to segregate from the less advantaged, means the system is failing some vulnerable groups. This has an impact on student potential: 'Right now, you could be extremely talented but if you come to a school with poor standards and your parents don't know what choices you have, then you won't ever develop those talents.'

Since independent schools have very limited powers of selection, and no powers for selecting on the basis of background, ethnic, religious or otherwise, a major factor causing these forms of selection must be self-selection by families. In other words, independent schools attract more active participants in the education sector because pupils are not sent to them unless a specific choice is made. Kallstenius also suspects that independent schools use indirect methods of selection: 'not all students are looked on as attractive. By law they are not allowed to select but they might encourage easier students to come. For example, which homes do they send marketing material to, which newspapers do they advertise in? They calculate which sort of pupils they will get by marketing to particular areas.'

Stawström, of the Swedish Association of Independent Schools, disputes this contention. He claims that in general independent schools try to appeal to parents in the surrounding district and that the resulting homogeneity is likely due to neighbourhood segregation, especially within the Stockholm area. Mats Gerdau, Moderate party parliamentary representative, concurs: 'The main problem is segregation by neighbourhoods. Previously, you had people kept hostage [by the school system] where they lived.'

Preventing segregation

When it comes to tackling segregation, the key answer on everyone's lips is more information. The right to choose is already out there and has been framed in a very equitable manner. It is now a matter of closing the gap between those who actively choose to make the best of the education system and those who do not because they do not know how or even that they can. Equality of opportunity needs to be transformed into equality of access. Kallstenius: 'One very important question concerns information to ensure that all parents know how to use the choice and know which alternatives they have. It should not depend on where you live or your background whether you can make a good choice.'

'We emphasise more information,' Bergström echoes. He feels that it is not just those that have yet to use the school choice system that will benefit but also those that already are using it: 'The bad side of [school choice] is that there are schools that have introduced all kinds of strange courses, often at high school [upper secondary] level – especially media. Things like how to become a pop star. Things that are not that good, actually… In order to make students more aware of the long-term consequences of their choices, we need to introduce new performance criteria.'

Bergström suggests one way in which more information should be available in the future. It includes a role for government in not just setting minimum curriculum standards (as Skolverket currently does), but also offering a form of independent supervision of standards. Similar to the nominal purpose of league tables and Ofsted inspections in the UK, it would be essential not to allow short-term political interests to influence these observers: 'Their focus should be on the best possible education for students and the economy in the long run. You would need high credibility institutions responsible for such an organisation.'

Besides this, Bergström envisages that once there is a critical mass of parents making a choice, there will be more spontaneous development of school comparison websites managed by parents and guides written by independent companies, offering the example of 'SchoolMatters', a service provided by Standard and Poor's in the US.[41]

Gerdau believes that more rigorous assessment and testing at the municipal and national level will also play a role in building up more information: 'The main reason why we have many schools that are not performing so well is that we are not evaluating them from the beginning.' Sweden currently has relatively few national exams compared to Britain, although that is now set to change. Even national exam scripts are usually marked by class teachers and not anonymously. This means there is a greater chance of variation between test scores for pupils of similar standards. As in the UK, there is also the problem of grade inflation taking place across the whole system. A policy of more stringent test control is meant to weed this out, allowing information about school performance to be less ambiguous.

In his own district, Nacka, Mats Gerdau and the local Moderate Party have taken the competitive line one step further by introducing compulsory school choice. A form is sent out to all parents with a brochure describing the municipal and independent schools in the district. They use an optional online registration system to make it easy for everyone to make an active choice: 'I don't put anyone in a school except my own children; all parents have to choose. But we have to make it easier for them to choose. In Nacka we have a brochure of schools, in different languages, and on the Web... 90 per cent [of families] make a choice after the first letter is sent out. Then by the time we have done a reminder, about 10 or 15 individual families haven't made an active choice.' By doing this, Gerdau intends to make the new options unambiguous to everyone, regardless of background, and to get more people using the system.

As for dealing with the widening gap in school performance across the system, Gerdau advocates more robust competition for municipal schools: 'We should not have a wide gap. It is not a problem that good schools are getting better. It is that we have some schools not performing well and you need to raise their quality. If students choose to leave the bad schools [and] select better schools, the solution has to be to close down bad schools. But this is a hard decision for a municipality. It is a failure to close down a school, and they have been holding off on doing it.'

Of course, while allowing failed schools to shut is one part of school choice, it benefits no one without giving municipal schools the ability to adapt and innovate to prevent that happening. One method of achieving this is to apply the same funding mechanisms and freedoms that independent schools have: 'In Nacka, we introduced a voucher system for municipal schools as well. They choose how to apply their funds which are given per pupil.'

Gerdau cites one particular example of a municipal school, Internationella skolan (ISN), situated in one of the poorest areas of Nacka. It has developed an innovative international profile with half of all classes conducted in English (similar to the English International School chain of independent schools). This has served a mix of different communities in the local area, and gone on to attract pupils from richer Swedish backgrounds outside that local area to create an even more diverse set of pupils.

The competitive model has been shown to work too. Nacka has significantly higher average test scores than the rest of Sweden, but more importantly, there is now no difference at all between standards in independent schools and municipal schools. In 2006, both the total school assessment average score and the municipal school assessment average score for school leavers in Nacka were 231; this compared to the national municipal school average of 205.3, and even beating the national independent school average of 225.3. This suggests that better schools do not mean fewer municipal schools (83 per cent of Nacka's compulsory school leavers are from municipal schools), but merely schools of any sort operating with the same increased freedoms and responsibilities that independent schools have. It is in these circumstances that we see school choice driving both improved outcomes *and* equity simultaneously.

Where municipal schools take on the same innovative attitude as their competing independent schools, to parents it becomes no longer a question of whether they choose a municipal or independent school but what sort of features they are looking for in any school, independent or not. This shows that there is nothing inherently inefficient about a state owned school so long as it is subject to the same competitive structures as independent schools. This is the long-term solution favoured by Gerdau and many other Moderates to the problems of segregation and differentiated standards between schools. As he concludes: 'the solution is not less competition but more'.

Controversy over for-profit schools

For-profit schools are a particularly radical element of this reform and they have come under additional scrutiny and attack from the Left in Sweden. In August 2006, the Swedish Democratic Party pledged in their manifesto to prevent school companies from issuing profits to shareholders.[42] There are two common arguments for opposing for-profit companies. The first is a practical argument: any money being issued as profits to a company owner or shareholders is obviously not being spent on pupils' education. The argument goes that even if parents are happy to use the school and teachers are happy to teach and standards are acceptable, there must be some loss in the system. Some would refer to this as exploitation. The second argument is more from principle: this claims that *even if* standards offered by for-profit schools are as good as or better than their non-profit and state counterparts, it is wrong for public funds to allow private individuals to be enriched.

Stawström tackles the first point explaining that for-profit companies are just as interested in delivering a better standard of education as everyone else. He suggests that companies do not get the same level of return in this sector as they do in most other areas. As a consequence, even successful for-profit schools are more like social enterprises: 'one big company, John Bauer, processed SEK 1.8 billion in the last few years. Out of that they have used only SEK 1.7 billion to run the schools, with a profit of SEK 100 million [around £8 million]. That is less than 6 per cent. A normal company would not accept profit margins like that... it is very small money comparatively.' In other words, with strictly capped fees, few companies can make a profit at all after reinvesting into the school chain. Those that do make profits, make a relatively modest amount, especially compared to initial investment. This makes education more of a market for social enterprise rather than pure commerce.

Stawström also suggests that the fact that some companies can make profits is not so much a problem for them, but rather shows up their non-profit competition: 'since we have these operators that are getting bigger and bigger and bigger, small figures in percentages look very big in aggregate and the ordinary Swede does not like the idea of people taking a cut like that. Somewhere someone is making money. How do these operations make some money on the bottom line? Because they run their schools very well. That is the problem with municipal schools; they don't look after the money.'

Sandström has taken on the principle of the second argument by pointing out 'the incoherence of allowing profits for companies selling books and other supplies, building or letting school buildings, or indeed from being a teacher, all using public money, while objecting to companies making profits from the actual running of schools'.[43] In other words, the argument on the Left against profits is not so much principled as ideological. They have no qualms with teachers 'profiting' from teaching; they do not ask teachers to volunteer their labour or accept a small stipend only. Rather it is opposition to the institution of shareholder companies operating in a market.

In the case of the UK, in particular, far more dangerous precedents have already been set than simply allowing for profit companies *to offer* education to families. For example, many educational institutions use Capita for criminal records checks, allowing a for-profit company to exploit a privileged position in a bureaucracy with which to siphon off state funds from the school system when new members of staff have to be appointed. In addition, the global publisher, Pearson Education, has acquired the UK's largest exam board, Edexcel.[44] Due to the prime position that Edexcel holds in the 'assessment' market, state schools are almost compelled to use their services and thereby enrich a large corporation, which has bought its way into a position of power over state institutions. This is the worst of both worlds as commercial operations have been welcomed into the British education sector but not in a way that encourages them to compete for customers: commerce without choice. By contrast, in Sweden, companies only have a hope of making any money at all by appealing directly to families, who always have the option of rejecting their services on any grounds. So in Sweden, using a for-profit company is just one option of many. In the UK, for some it is already compulsory.

In the end, the argument over for-profit companies rests not so much on questions of efficiency and performance on the ground so much as the place of profit making institutions within the ideological framework of policy makers. It seems unlikely that a consensus on this element of school choice will be reached soon in favour of for-profit schools, even though it appears to be important in Sweden to spurring the expansion of high performing schools. But even if a political consensus is impossible to reach, perhaps all sides of the debate will at least endorse the benefits of a more general decentralised system, or social market. As Bergström sums up: 'The money used to come from above, besides all kinds of directives, but when they changed to the voucher system, that changed to a focus on what parents and students want.'

2

The Challenge for School Reform
in England

There are several problems with education provision in the UK. However, before delving into those problems it is worth noting that internationally we are not in particularly bad shape, at least when we look at our position in snapshot. Depending on the measure, we rank midway in the league table of developed countries and that is with a total expenditure on education that ranks a little below the OECD average. Education in England as a whole can by no means be described as 'world class', but neither is it a catastrophe. The problem is that, while our position internationally is respectable, there is evidence to suggest that England's current trend points downwards. This is not just relative compared to other countries, but also in absolute levels of education. In other words, by some measures we are not just falling behind as international competition catches up, we are even losing ground to our previous standards as well. More importantly, this drop in standards impacts disproportionately on children from lower socio-economic backgrounds, reflecting a 'long tail' in educational outcomes where some people in England do very well while others experience outcomes that are amongst the worst in Europe.

The latest results from PISA,[1] an OECD administered project that compares education standards across developed nations, offers a case in point. These results are based on testing 15-year-olds, which offers a relatively good indicator of the average standards of students who will soon be entering the workplace and tertiary education. In 2006, in maths the United Kingdom ranked 24th in PISA's international rankings with 495 points compared to a 498-point international average. That is a 34-point decline from 2000 when our score was 529 and we were ranked eighth. Similarly, in reading, the UK ranks 17th with a score of 495 compared to the international average of 492. In 2000, the UK was ranked seventh and scored 523.

Results from the Progress in International Literacy Study (PIRLS)[2] suggest a similar trend in the reading ability of ten-year-olds. England's mean score fell from 553 in 2001 to 539 in 2006. This comparison between years cannot be taken as certain. It depends on the method used to link the results of the tests from 2001 to 2006 and there is some suggestion that the 2001 results were overstated to begin with through poor sampling of pupils. However, the results certainly demonstrate that England's primary reading results have remained static while many other countries continue to improve. This leaves us some way behind Sweden, Germany, Italy, Luxembourg, even Hungary and Bulgaria. England dropped in the league of 40 countries taking part from being third in 2001 to 19th in 2006.

Of rather greater concern is what PIRLS suggests about the wide distribution of reading abilities. England has what could be described as a 'long tail' of reading under-achievement: i.e. not only are average reading abilities not what they could be, but also reading abilities within normal pupil distributions vary widely. While the overall mean is 539, the 25th quartile is significantly below the international average of 500, while seven per cent of pupils in England failed to pass even the lowest international benchmark of 400.[3] As a consequence, England has some of the most literate children in the world; yet it also has some of the most illiterate in the developed world.

This is not a new problem facing Britain. Indeed according to most studies available, the level of illiteracy amongst school children has remained stable since 1948,[4] although the changing demands in the workplace clearly make this situation less and less tolerable for those unable to read or write. This is underlined by a recent report from Cambridge University and the University of London that suggests Britain's economic productivity is lagging precisely because young people are lacking basic knowledge of the 'three Rs'.[5]

There are far greater ramifications than simple productivity in the workplace, however. As argued in a previous Civitas report,[6] poor basic literacy skills are likely to be a crucial factor in Britain's comparative lack of social mobility: the potential for people from low income families to gain a better level of education and improve their job prospects. The Sutton Trust has found that intergenerational mobility declined significantly from 1958 to 1970 and that from 1970 to 2000 has remained at the same stagnant level. In fact, the relationship between parental income and expected outcomes for children actually strengthened over that period.[7] At the same time, the so-called 'education gap' has, according to an Institute of Education report, expanded over the last 20 years, with the majority of newly available university places going to children of middle-class families.[8] In contrast, nearly 80 per cent of pupils eligible for free school meals (mostly children from working-class back-grounds) are failing to achieve five GCSEs at grades A* to C, including English and maths, the government's preferred basic measure of achievement at secondary school.[9] We can deduce from this that there are entire sectors of society missing out both on the opportunity for higher education and (perhaps more significantly) skilled occupations, because primary and secondary education is failing to provide them with the pre-requisite basic skills.

Hence, perhaps now more than ever in the last half-century, children from poor backgrounds appear to have significantly worse academic and career outcomes than those from advantaged backgrounds. This lack of mobility in turn entrenches differences between social classes, and means that the life chances of individuals come to be defined more by circumstance than by talent or effort. It is highly likely that this downward spiral in education in some communities also plays a major role in alienating children from society, attacking their personal aspirations, and making them unhappy generally, as witnessed by a damning 2007 Unicef report on child well-being that ranked the UK bottom in a list of OECD countries.[10] The challenge for school reform, more than just to improve schools generally, is to tackle the differences in educational outcomes and, thereby, contribute to improving the lives of children more generally.

Why is this happening?

How is it that the education sector in England is delivering such a poor standard of education to a significant proportion of children? There are, of course, many reasons, but the main contention of this report is that at the heart of the problem lies a state-maintained sector that is currently beholden to bureaucratic interests rather than to the interests of parents and children. The reason for this is, just like Sweden before their school choice reforms, investment is directed from above with very little input from the parents and children who actually use the system, and in many cases even the head teachers who have to make it function. The facts of this are neatly illustrated in the two main ways that government interacts with the system: how it applies funding to education and how it measures the outcomes. On both these fronts, the government is unable to achieve the desired focus on the needs of individual pupils.

The headline figures for investment under Labour are impressive. Since 2000/2001, real terms UK expenditure on education has risen from £52.8 billion to an estimated £69.4 billion in 2007/2008. Revenue expenditure per-pupil has risen, according to official government figures, from £3,690 to £5,500 over the same period.[11] But how much of this money is really filtering down through Whitehall into schools and eventually to individual pupils? There are, unfortunately, a great many ways that funds can be siphoned off into projects with dubious outcomes under such a centralised system. Obviously, investment has to be directed and regulated so that it gets spent on areas where there is a lack of provision. The problem for any government is identifying those areas from their relatively distant position. It does not help that ministers have to keep a watchful eye on news headlines and face constant pressure to announce major investment programmes to quell public disquiet on particular issues as they arise.

This creates a tendency to use ring-fenced funds for specific knee-jerk projects rather than pushing investment decisions right to the frontline where it can be applied to what is most useful in schools. In the month of January 2008 alone, the Department for Children, Schools and Families announced projects worth £727.5 million (besides various uncosted projects), which included everything from boosting maths and science teaching through providing cheap Internet access to parents, to a campaign to raise standards in London schools.[12] These projects, eye-catching and impressive as they are, are unlikely to be met with identical success across the school system. Some schools might well benefit, for example, from their pupils having more access to the Internet, while others might not.

However, that sort of question is not a school's decision any more: the pledge has already been made and a cohort of civil servants deployed to achieve it. If something is a government policy then that is what schools are required to provide, whether it is useful in a particular context or not.

A consequence of this form of investment is the proliferation of arms-length education agencies operating at the national level, which take up a hefty proportion of government investment in education. According to the Economic Research Council, in 2001 total expenditure on quangos associated with the Department for Education and Skills was £8.4 billion. No small sum, but by 2006, that figure had more than doubled to £18.7 billion.[13] Big spenders include the Learning and Skills Council, the Training and Development Agency for Schools and the Qualifications and Curriculum Authority. Of course, some of the work being conducted by these national agencies is necessary, but one wonders whether schools themselves might be in a better position to decide what training, development and guidance they need from outside agencies rather than ministers and civil servants.

The measurement of outcomes, through qualifications and assessment, demonstrates rather more clearly how the system tends to focus on priorities set centrally. Test results are clearly only one element of educational outcomes. They are, however, currently the only measurable outcomes that are available on a system-wide level. So although they are used heavily in this analysis, they should only ever be considered as *indicators* of achievement rather than proof. Indeed, it has often exacerbated problems in education that exam results have been treated as equivalent to achievement.

It is fascinating to note how national exam results stand out in marked contrast to the international evidence on standards. Restricting one's view deliberately to national exams gives the impression that the last decade has seen a phenomenal improvement in school standards. For example, in 1997, 46.3 per cent of GCSE students at the end of compulsory education achieved five or more A*-C grades while 6.6 per cent had no passes. By 2006, 58.5 per cent of pupils achieved five or more grades A*-C, while only 2.2 per cent did not achieve any passes.[14] Similarly, in 1997, 87.2 per cent of A-level entries were passes: by 2006, this was the case for 97.2 per cent of the entries. Meanwhile, the percentage of A-grades rose from 16.1 per cent to 24.1 per cent.[15]

Unsurprisingly these exam results have become the backdrop to many optimistic ministerial pronouncements over the years. Yet there is something amiss in these results and it is not necessary to look even to international evidence to see that they are not the harbingers of spectacular improvements, as ministers like to suggest. The Curriculum Evaluation Management (CEM) centre at Durham University conducts independent studies of pupil abilities, with test standards kept as stable as possible. This allows exam standards to be compared from year to year so that it is possible to see how much students have really improved over that time scale.

The latest results available from the YELLIS test (the CEM's test of mathematical and verbal abilities) denote a very small improvement in the basic abilities of pupils from 1995 to 2006. They do, however, note a much larger change in what pupils of the same basic abilities gain at GCSE. A student who scored 45 (just below the average) on the YELLIS test could expect to achieve D-grades in French, maths and history at GCSE in 1996, but by 2006 would be receiving C grades. This is sufficient to push a number of students into achieving the five grades at A*-C benchmark, the government's current (but minimal) measure of success.

Taking an average of 26 subjects, pupils of the same YELLIS standard could generally expect to achieve around half-a-grade higher in 2006 than they could in 1996.[16]

The differences are rather greater at A-level. Results from the ALIS project (the A-level equivalent to YELLIS) uses the International Test of Developed Abilities to compare the attainment of pupils from year to year. Taking an average of 40 A-level subjects, Robert Coe found that those scoring 50 per cent on the ITDA test in 1997 would tend to achieve low C-grades, but by 2005 were achieving low B-grades. Essentially, a B-grade of today is worth, in general ability terms, the C-grade of around ten years ago.[17]

Were this simply a matter of grade inflation resulting in the same qualifications not being comparable from year to year, this issue would be of little concern. But the problem is not grade inflation in itself but what it shows about the education system. What has happened is that proficiency at passing GCSEs and A-levels has become progressively detached from general abilities that are useful for higher education, employment and life skills generally. This would be considered more of a problem, were the priorities of the system to develop the knowledge and abilities of pupils. But it is not. In a case of the tail wagging the dog, the ability to pass the exams *themselves* has become the priority and the thing for teachers and pupils to concentrate on. Unfortunately, the ability to pass a specific set of exams at the ages of 16 and 18 does not, in itself, contribute to real economic productivity or happiness and fulfilment in life.

GCSEs and A-levels, the current official indicators of what makes a good school and what defines a successful pupil, are bad measures of how well pupils are doing. Yet the government treats exam results as a proxy for school productivity, with the Department for Schools, Children and Families, the Qualifications and Curriculum Authority and the Office for Standards in Education (Ofsted) placing primary emphasis on good exam results representing success and achievement. Under this regime the actual skills and abilities of pupils come to be disregarded.

This problem becomes more acute when the interests of pupils come to be directly at odds with the interests of the school as judged by the exam and assessment system. The continual drive to improve results creates a damaging incentive for schools to find qualifications that are likely to produce good results with the least amount of effort and talent. General National Vocational Qualifications (GNVQs) taken at the same time as and often in lieu of GCSEs offers perhaps the most widely used 'loophole' used to drive up standards on paper while not actually tackling student's educational outcomes. Professor Smithers of the University of Buckingham's Centre for Education and Employment Research found that thousands of students took courses in these 'quasi-academic' subjects, which include science, information and communication technology and business. However, 'entry to the more practically-sounding fields is miniscule. Hospitality and catering, manufacturing, construction, retail and distributive trades, land and environment together account for only 1.2 per cent of the Intermediate GNVQ'. Indeed, over half of all the GNVQs taken are in the single subject, ICT. Smithers has also noted that the influence these subjects have had on results is significant: 'from 2001 the proportion achieving five good GCSEs themselves has plateaued at about 50 per cent and the increase [up to 2005] has been through intermediate GNVQs which count as four GCSEs'.[18] David Brown, a retired head teacher, calculated that since GNVQs are valued so highly compared to GCSEs, studying the ICT GNVQ was 13 times as effective in boosting a school's league table position as studying maths.[19]

A-levels have suffered a similar commute to easier subjects that appear to offer improved results for schools. From 1996 to 2007, the number of A-level entries has increased by nearly 100,000. However, this increase has not been reflected in traditional subjects. In fact, many have declining numbers of entries: physics, French and German have all registered reductions of more than 4,000, 10,000 and 3,000 respectively. By contrast, psychology has increased by 30,000; media & film studies by 16,000 and PE by nearly 12,000.[20]

Officially, qualifications in all A-level subjects are worth exactly the same but, as Peter Tymms and Robert Coe of Durham University have demonstrated, some A-level subjects are less demanding than others: 'It is perfectly clear from our research that two A-levels are not equal, with some more severely graded than others.' Their research found that students with Bs in GCSE history, economics, geography, English language and literature, sociology and business studies went on to attain C on average in the same subjects at A-level. However, Coe and Tymms found that those with Bs in GCSE maths, computing, German, French, chemistry, physics and biology were more likely to get Ds at A-level.[21]

The result is not just a case of students themselves choosing easier subjects. There is evidence that some schools have been actively discouraging pupils from taking subjects that are deemed more challenging and are therefore less 'safe' for league table purposes. An ICM survey commissioned by the Association of Colleges in 2006 showed that 55 per cent of students felt that teachers steer them towards courses in which their school does best, rather than what they needed.[22]

It is hard to predict exactly what the long-term consequences of disregarding challenging subjects will be, but a number of experts have described their fears. Richard Pike, chief executive of the Royal Society of Chemistry, has argued that schools are discouraging students from taking maths A-level. He noted: 'This contrasts starkly with countries like China, in which mathematics is seen as integral to the sciences and to the nation's economy.'[23]

David Hart, then general secretary of the National Association of Head Teachers, argued that 'soft' subjects may be helping students get into higher education but that 'in the long term I'm not sure it does very much for their career prospects'.[24] Robert Kirby-Harris, chief executive of the Institute of Physics, has also argued that exams present a 'crazy situation' in which A-level students are opting for subjects which have 'poor career prospects'.[25] In addition, Kathleen Tattersall, chair of the Institute of Education Assessors, has described how history, in particular, is becoming an endangered subject as more students opt for subjects such as media studies and photography.[26]

The irony is that this focus on exam results and regulated assessment is meant to ensure high standards of teaching in all schools, but the flaws in the system have created incentives that act to undermine standards and to direct the efforts of both teachers and pupils in the wrong direction. Of course, there are still very good teachers and some very good schools in the maintained sector, and there are many successful pupils. However, the structures and incentives operating at the centre are working against those successful outcomes rather than for them. It means, for example, that when a school begins to struggle, its first priority is not to concentrate on getting genuinely better outcomes for their pupils, but on creating better outcomes on paper, the ones that are acceptable to the central bureaucracy.

Hence, the very mechanism designed to assure some quality in every school has led, when implemented systematically, to a lower quality of education being generated in practice. Consequently, the system reacts badly to the real demands of parents and needs of children, causing those that are able to seek better education elsewhere. It is this behaviour that accounts in large part for the current imbalance in outcomes between the rich and the poor: middle-class families are more successful at appropriating quality education for their children. Having found that the education on offer 'free at the point of use' is inadequate (or risks becoming adequate), these families attempt to do what they would do in any other case of scarcity or failure: they seek out alternatives.

One well-documented method is to seek out better schools within the state maintained sector. In this respect, middle-class parents use the (currently highly constrained) provision for school choice already offered by the school admissions system. As a recent Institute for Public Policy Research report has shown, state maintained schools are more segregated than their surrounding neighbourhoods. The effects are particularly felt in densely populated areas where the difference between local schools is most tangible: 'Different neighbourhoods are strongly segregated by social class and income, and this is reflected in the attainment of pupils from different areas. However, schools are significantly more segregated than neighbourhoods, especially in densely populated urban areas where more schools are within reasonable travelling distance. These findings are replicated for income (as indicated by entitlement to free school meals) as well as for prior ability, and London is particularly strongly affected.'[27]

How do middle-class families manage to manipulate the system so successfully that they end up clustering in good schools? To an extent, it is the very complexity of admissions that is the greatest asset to the families with 'voice'. Weighing in at a hefty 127 pages, the frequently altered

School Admissions Code is packed full of entitlements, rights and responsibilities designed to 'create a schools system shaped by parents which delivers excellence and equity, developing the talents and potential of every child, regardless of their background; a system where all parents feel they have the same opportunities to apply for the schools they want for their child'.[28] Yet the result is to create a set of rules so baroque that it is now not even clear to many head teachers what constitutes legitimate admissions practice.[29] In this context, with the rules being difficult enough to interpret so as to make the rights of families ambiguous, it seems likely that the parents who make a fuss are more likely to be better served. The rule of the bureaucratic jungle: 'survival of the loudest'.

Much of this difficultly comes from the fact that different rules apply to different sorts of schools. A child has a general right to attend any school in the state sector so long as there is a place available (a surprisingly similar right to that offered to children in Sweden). The system struggles, as one would expect, when a school is oversubscribed with more pupils wanting to attend the school than there are places available, often where the other schools in the area are known by parents to be inadequate. In such cases, schools are meant to develop a fair method of selection, which might include the use of catchment areas, ability banding or lotteries. However, there are so many allowable deviations to this general practice that the exceptions almost become the rule. Schools that specialise in particular subject areas (like arts, sport or science) are permitted to select a proportion of their pupils on the basis of 'aptitude' for their specialism. In addition, faith schools, which are frequently oversubscribed, are permitted to select pupils on the basis of religious background and observance. These selection procedures are particularly controversial since they often appear to amount to selection by ability by proxy. In addition, there are still grammar schools in some counties that are permitted to select entirely by ability.

To complicate matters further, while the local education authority usually regulates access to ordinary maintained schools, some sorts of schools, including City Technology Colleges, Academies and voluntary aided (usually faith) schools, are their own admission authorities. As Stephen Ball of the Institute of Education at the University of London has argued, this proliferation of new types of school with their own admissions procedures merely serves to create 'new opportunities for middle-class parents to seek social advantage'.[30] Philip Hunter, the chief schools adjudicator, who oversees admissions, has commented that 'advantaged middle-class parents will always find ways of advancing their cases'.[31]

Besides that, state education does not function in a vacuum; more affluent families also have the choice to send their children to independent schools. Britain, unlike Sweden before the 1992 reform, already has a growing independent schools sector. According to the 2008 Independent Schools Council census, over 671,000 pupils attend independent schools, nearly seven per cent of total UK pupils.[32] It is well established that fee-paying independent schools perform better than maintained schools. Over one in four grades awarded at GCSE to independent school pupils are A*, while over half are A or A*, compared to 6.3 per cent and 19.1 per cent (respectively) nationally.[33] The difference is almost as stark when it comes to A-level results: 50 per cent of A-level grades in the independent sector are at grade A compared to a national average of 25.3 per cent.[34] While it is dangerous to rely on such national exams as an appropriate proxy for real achievement, the Sutton Trust has found that independent schools in England also perform phenomenally well according to international comparisons: 'The UK's independent schools, which obtained the highest overall score for a school group on reading in PISA 2000, were second only to Korea in maths in PISA 2003, 86 points ahead of the state schools.'[35]

Moreover, this is only the tip of the iceberg in terms of demand for better education than what the state has to offer. A Mori survey found in 2004 that half of all parents would send their children to an independent school if they could afford it.[36] Those who cannot afford independent schools continue to pursue other options. It is estimated that around a quarter of all children taking GCSEs receive private tuition to supplement their mainstream schoolwork.[37] But private tutoring is expensive, with many families being prepared to pay up to £40 per hour for tuition. Fees of £80 per hour for tutors who are in particular demand are not unheard of.

As a consequence, there are other popular forms of independent provision for education besides fully-fledged schools and private tutors. The DfES estimated that there are around 5,000 supplementary schools. Kumon, for example, is one large chain of such schools that concentrates on teaching the basics of maths and English. It has 550 schools that together teach 48,000 students in the UK. Their fee is £85 a month for tuition in both subjects. On the far end of this spectrum of choices, parents still retain the right to educate their own children away from either independent or state provision in home schools for which systematic surveys are currently lacking.

The education debate

These problems with the current education system are accepted to different extents across the political spectrum: an over-centralised system fails to provide an adequate level of education to all the pupils using it and bogs down teachers and staff in bureaucratic requirements and guidelines. Meanwhile, middle-class parents exploit any open aspects of the system, such as school choice, faith schools and independent schools, to get ahead. The main area of controversy is what to do about this situation. The problem is that the debate up until now has tended to be polarised along lines that do not really discuss the essential aspects of the system: how open or closed it should be, how local or how centralised. It tends to assume the status quo in this respect and the main discussion has become about what policies government should enforce from above rather than whether a particular issue should be the responsibility of government in the UK.

The Left

The traditional Left position has tended to concentrate on closing what they see as loopholes by which the middle classes exploit the system. They consider school choice to be a problem exacerbating poor performance under the current system rather than a potential solution with which to drive up standards. Sarah Tough and Richard Brooks, writing for IPPR, believe the answer is for the admissions system to be standardised so that no school gets to be the guardian of its own admissions. In the long term, they advocate that the current system of parent preference tempered by consideration of catchment area and elements of selection should be overhauled and turned into a system of 'fair banding', under which every school has a representative mix of pupils of different abilities representing the whole pupil population. This would set parental preference as a low priority since, essentially, being able to choose a school because it offers a better standard of education would be banned under such a system. If applied throughout the whole system, this would effectively lead to the end of grammar schools. The current Labour government seems to support these ideas. A recent report by the National Centre for Social Research and Sheffield Hallam University and funded by the DCSF has set out plans to strip all schools of powers to select pupils and force them to accept quotas of pupils of various abilities.[38]

The other main area that the Left has traditionally targeted is the part of the education sector previously out of reach of government altogether: independent schools. Sunder Katwala, general secretary of the Fabian Society, in a recent speech on life chances and social mobility called for 'a rational debate about the impact of private education'. He advocates a re-think of the public benefit that independent schools offer that justifies their charitable status and, even more radically, putting value added tax on school fees to 'finance an opportunity fund to tackle educational disadvantage'.[39] Under the auspices of the Charity Commission, this policy too is now being pursued. Independent schools are now subject to a stricter 'public benefit' test which the Charity Commission has suggested could be passed by having lower fees, providing free or subsidised places and sharing their resources with the community.[40]

In concentrating on this area, the Left have doubtless identified an aspect of the current system that exacerbates inequality but there are several problems with this singular approach to reform. The main intention behind it is to remove the current advantages that middle-class children have over less advantaged pupils. In this respect, it will fail. These policies fail to recognise that, useful as grammar schools, faith schools and fee-paying independent schools are to middle-class families, they are a symptom rather than a cause of this growing educational apartheid.

The real reason behind these advantages is rather more difficult to fathom. Middle-class families are tenacious in their pursuit of superior education for their children. Average independent school fees are now more than £10,000 per annum, and those who cannot afford that level of investment, would if they could. They make up for the standards shortfall by using tutors, supplementary education and their own time and resources. Just making those choices moderately more expensive cannot stop that behaviour, and standing up to a cultural phenomenon that is so heavily ingrained within the middle classes is (even for a government) like commanding the Atlantic tides to cease. It would be impossible to prohibit middle-class parents from trying to improve the life chances of their own children without essentially changing what it means to be middle-class. Besides those practical concerns, it is also a tremendous shame, and waste, to have a government policy aimed at inhibiting parents' ability to improve the life chances of their children. Even if the motivation is noble and egalitarian, the result can only reduce the number of well-educated children. What is more urgently needed is a reform that will offer the same advantages that middle-class children already have to those from less advantaged backgrounds, a policy of levelling up rather than levelling down.

The underlying issue is that the Left has traditionally tended to look at the successes of the current system, independent schools, grammar schools and even the over-subscribed comprehensives and see them, perversely, as the cause of the problem—the schools that achieve are defined as the ones in need of 'reform'. What these policy positions do not contain is much idea of how to improve the remainder of the education sector once the successful elements of it have been 'reformed' or abolished. The main idea up until now was, quite simply, more investment in schools. However, that is reliant on the ability to find more money to invest in education from the treasury and spending it wisely. Under the current economic circumstances, this solution is likely to become increasingly difficult.

This lack of examination of the structural flaws in the system is perhaps part of an ideological blind spot, the assumption that all a state-funded education system requires is ever more investment to improve standards and that any shortfall in standards must be due to under-investment rather than poor management. The idea that there might be something inherently damaging about a system that deploys pupils into centrally managed schools that are compelled to pursue (ever-changing) government ends, has not yet been embraced by the mainstream Left. This is surprising considering how historically sceptical the Left have been of the ability of government to look after the genuine interests of children's education. Yet the international evidence seems to be pointing increasingly in that direction, as the Sutton Trust suggests: 'An unpalatable lesson for governments from the OECD/PISA studies may be that schools are better off without their close attention... independent schools and government-funded private schools generally obtained better results, irrespective of the social background of the intakes, than government-run schools. A likely explanation is that these schools do not continually have government on their backs.'[41]

By contrast, their report suggests there is little apparent correlation between admissions, the Left's preferred bugbear, and performance: '... none of the main methods of school admission was significantly associated with a country's performance in the PISA 2003 maths tests. Whether school admission was by proximity, by previous performance, or by one of the other methods did not make a sufficient difference to show up in the national results.'[42]

The main problem for the Left is that it targets good schools for attracting the best pupils but does not offer an effective systematic mechanism to improve failing schools. They put equality in the state system before good outcomes, a policy that, ironically, can only harm the disadvantaged since they disproportionately have to rely entirely on state education. More to the point, as we have seen in Sweden, there need not be *any* compromise between good outcomes for individual pupils and greater equality.

The Right

The Right has its own problems with education policy. Although school choice has played a role in theoretical discussion, this has not filtered down into a systematic Conservative Party policy. Indeed, Conservative policy in the 1980s and 1990s followed the 'managerialist' model of principles of so-called 'organisational excellence' enforced by guidelines and inspections. It was the Conservatives who introduced the National Curriculum in 1988 and thereby set the precedent for central government creating statutory guidance on what topics should be taught throughout the entire school sector, as well as what methods should be used. The government's stranglehold on schools was further increased in 1992 by the introduction of government target setting and the Office for Standards in Education (Ofsted). As Civitas has found, these institutions have since become implicated in the politicisation of the education sector, making teachers more beholden to government priorities.[43] Ofsted has even been used to harass successful schools, including independent schools, that fail to follow the government's prescribed teaching methods.[44]

The deregulating elements of the 1988 Education Reform Act were, therefore, more the exception than the rule in Conservative policy. These allowed families to express a direct preference for a school other than their local one and, if there was a space available, to attend. This 'open enrolment' reform was, unfortunately, not matched with supply-side deregulation (allowing new schools to enter the sector). This meant that rather than having schools competing for pupils, the perverse result was more pupils competing for limited school places. It is highly doubtful that giving parents a preference in this context has driven up standards through competition, but what is more certain is that it has contributed to segregation within the school system, a major problem that only the Left has fully appreciated.

Underlying this issue is the way that the Right have tended to conflate pupil selection with choice. It is not parent choice that the Right have explicitly supported so much as a school's choice of pupils, whether by faith or by competitive selection. Of course, this policy can be described, in a sense, as 'school choice', because faith schools and grammar schools tend to be popular with parents. The problem is that this sort of school choice, based on competitive selection and school-regulated admissions, means that many pupils are denied places at better schools. One pupil's choice is another pupil's denial of choice, meaning there are winners and losers in the chase for the good places. As a recent Sheffield Hallam University/ National Centre for Social Research study found, 19 per cent of parents are dissatisfied with the choice of schools available and 15 per cent of parents (28 per cent in London) do not get their child into their first choice school.[45] This dissatisfaction is a direct result of having formal parent choice while not allowing schools to adapt to those choices. This situation, though not so far tackled by Labour, was a Conservative construction.

A new consensus?

School choice, without the mechanism for new schools to open and adapt, turns admissions into a zero-sum game where middle-class families are the likely winners. It is not clear that the Right have taken on this particular lesson yet. As a consequence, it is worth noting that neither the Left nor the Right has ever endorsed unrestricted parent choice of schools and that both are actually in favour of selection, whether by the school or a local authority. The only disagreement has, at least traditionally, been the preferred pattern of selection, with the Right preferring competitive academic selection while the Left endorses bureaucratically imposed selection by mixed ability and social banding. The result so far has been an unsatisfactory and inconsistent compromise between the two positions, neither of which makes genuine parent choice a priority.

Sarah Tough and Richard Brooks, writing for IPPR, expressed the desire to get away from the recent Left/Right debate, characterised by: 'a dialogue of the deaf in which either "choice is good" or "selection is bad"'.[46] The solution to this stalemate is to synthesize these two contentions: 'Choice is good *and* selection is bad'. Policy should proceed on two fronts, to *extend* parent choice as far as possible and *reduce* selection as much as possible. A central policy pointer from the Sutton Trust implies a similar view: 'Schools should be given genuine autonomy, but within a framework which ensures equity.'[47]

The assumption up until now in Britain has been that choice and selection are almost interchangeable. Choice has implied schools having powers of selection that, in turn, entails that some parent choices are denied. What the Swedish reform has demonstrated is that this need not be the case, so long as the system of admissions focuses entirely on parent choice, and the supply of school places is elastic, expanding and contracting in line with parent choices. As the Swedish experience, and the district of Nacka in particular, has shown, a state-funded system that creates a social market in schools is the best mechanism for creating that provision of good school places. This way it is possible to create a system that respects the choice of every parent as a means to improve educational outcomes for all.

3

A School Choice Policy for England

The primary purpose of these policy recommendations is to sketch a framework to improve educational outcomes in the state maintained school sector, and especially to close some of the gap between the educational outcomes of the rich and poor. While one policy cannot begin to create the same outcomes across society, it can at least aim to prevent the schools system from being one of the generators of inequality. The assumption this policy operates on is that while differences in outcomes between schools have been exacerbated by segregation, they cannot be tackled by mere anti-segregationist policies. The mechanisms that have allowed differences in outcomes to emerge and become entrenched must be reformed.

School choice is an important tool in this respect. If applied systematically, the reform over a number of years will expand the availability of places in good schools. In turn, this will take the pressure off school admissions, and the urge amongst middle-class families to segregate will be reduced. By driving up standards in the whole sector, all schools will begin to appear more attractive to middle-class families, including those with more of a social mix. Hence, better performance will, in turn, reduce segregation. The intention is that this should contribute, in the long term, to an increase in social mobility.

This policy aims to generate two specific practical benefits in the short term already witnessed in Sweden that will work towards this primary purpose:

- New schools will offer higher standards of teaching and drive up standards at maintained schools by creating a greater diversity of schools available to all children in densely populated urban areas.

- Village schools currently threatened with closure due to their alleged economic inefficiency will be allowed to stay open as independent schools and manage their own budgets.

Evolution, not revolution

As discussed in chapter two, many of the problems in the current education system are caused by attempts at reform directed by central government that, whatever their original design, tend to take more autonomy away from teachers and disrupt the ordinary working of schools. The policy proposed here, aiming to achieve the same effect as in Sweden, will not directly affect existing schools, nor will it involve central government itself in opening any new schools. Instead, the underlying rules governing how new schools are established will be changed giving the policy continuity with the current system, while allowing changes on the ground to happen with a minimum of government interference.

Central government will not open any new schools under this reform, nor will any existing schools be closed or modified either. Insofar as any changes happen to the current system, the changes must happen in two distinct ways: to reduce the level of control that the government currently has within existing schools, and to reduce the level of selection that schools can make with respect to pupil admission. These changes should be made carefully, in a way that prevents disruption to existing structures but will eventually make them more equitable.

Use the structures already in place

Britain is in the advantageous position of already having in place many equivalent mechanisms to Sweden. In the final years of his term as Prime Minister, Tony Blair took an increasing interest in promoting choice and diversity within the school system. The result was a white paper, *Higher Standards, Better Schools for All* in 2005, and following that the Education and Inspections Act of 2006, which put in place several structures and initiatives designed to encourage more parent choice. Among them is the Office of the Schools Commissioner. According to the Department for Children, Schools and Families (DCSF), 'the Schools Commissioner challenges local authorities to provide a diverse range of schools to match the needs of their local area and to tackle poorly performing schools'.[1]

In essence, a government agency tasked with opening new schools under independent management already exists. The problem is the confined framework in which this agency and any independent suppliers have to operate. For example, although outside organisations are permitted to apply to set up or take over schools as academies or trusts, their ability to enact their own policy arrangements is very limited. They have to follow the National Curriculum and face inspections by Ofsted. Trusts, the most recent new school structure, have to form the same management structures required in every school. The DCSF even retains the right to remove managing trustees at the secretary of state's discretion and break up the trust. Setting up each school requires the consultation and permission of both central government and the local authority. The result is that any state schools under the current system cannot be independently owned and can barely be considered independently managed. It would be more accurate to describe the current process as adding another layer of management to an already heavily bureaucratic system.[2]

To open up provision, these structures can remain in place but the rules governing them must be changed significantly. The role of the Schools Commissioner should be altered so that it no longer, in the main, engages with other government departments. Instead, it should be the first and only point of access for any individual or group (including, charities, parent co-operatives, faith groups, companies and trusts) applying for permission to open a new school and receive public funds. These should include primary and secondary schools as well as sixth-form colleges and could be known as *Free schools* (analogous to the Swedish *friskolor*).

Local education authorities should also be permitted to apply for a school under their control to become Free. Schools that are not LEA controlled, including academies and voluntary aided schools, should also have the right to apply to become Free schools as well. However, the purpose of this is *not* to turn every school into a Free school, merely to make sure the option is there for LEAs and schools when it might be appropriate. In fact, the intention is that LEAs should retain greater control of community schools as central government becomes less engaged with direct provision.

Facilitating the opening of Free schools

Independent providers should be treated as entirely separate entities from the state. They should be allowed to have their own preferred management structure, set separate pay and conditions for their staff and own their own assets (including school premises if appropriate). One reason for this is that it would give confidence to outside investors (whether charitable or commercial) that assets associated with the school are protected from being directed according to central or local government budgets. Free schools should be exempt from Ofsted inspections. They should also be exempt from following the National Curriculum, although if they intend not to follow it, they should be required to provide significant detail of the curriculum they intend to teach when applying to the Schools Commissioner. Any permissible curriculum must develop skills in literacy and maths and at least half of all lessons must be taught in English (this requirement will still allow significant freedom for schools that wish to specialise in foreign and community language learning).

Free school applicants should have to conform to health and safety legislation, including child protection. They should have to describe the teaching methods they intend to employ, but variation should be permitted and even encouraged in this respect. They should describe the forms of assessment and qualifications the school will offer. While they should not be required to follow the ordinary national exam system, they will have to offer some form of checkable external assessment which is recognised by the Schools Commissioner. The range of assessment should be as flexible as possible, including national exams taken by other maintained schools, internationally recognised qualifications and established performance monitors like those offered by Durham University's Curriculum, Evaluation and Management Centre.

Applicants should make explicit the values (if any) that the Free school intends to teach, whether they are faith-based or secular. These must not conflict with respect for individual liberty and human rights. They should also have to demonstrate a robust policy on providing teaching staff with suitable qualifications for the provision of their pedagogy but this should not be limited to the current form of qualifications required in state schools. They should also demonstrate that there is some demand for a school of their type in the area they intend to establish (a list of interested parents would be sufficient) and have a sound financial plan. Although Free schools when first applying should have to describe the initial pupil capacity of the school, there should not be any limit placed on their expansion if there is demand for it.

Local authorities should have a 'right to reply' when an application is made to open a Free school in their district. However, the local authority should have no statutory authority to stop or even slow down an application. Their opinion should be sought explicitly to offer the Schools Commissioner their perspective on the application, not a right to veto a proposal. The application process should be designed to be as swift as possible so that new schools face few barriers to entry, with perhaps a target of having six weeks between the date of application and a decision. Established and successful Free school groups, if they emerge, should also be permitted to apply for a general right to open a new school with the same profile in any local authority whenever they have the resources.

The Schools Commissioner's role should be made more explicit under these rules, with a statutory duty to promote parent choice, diversity of school types and competition between different pedagogies. All the standards required for a successful application should be set out plainly and transparently, so that those who are well equipped to run a school can overcome these necessary bureaucratic barriers without being held up by unnecessary regulation. This would allow independent providers to concentrate on engaging with parents and their children rather than with arms of government. The assumption of the new system should be that if an application passes the standards required of the process, a school should be allowed to open and offer its form of education to parents unhindered by the Schools Commissioner, the Schools Adjudicator and the local education authority.

Moreover, LEA staff should be permitted to enter and observe the school in practice on a regular basis and should be required to do so in the first term to ensure that health and safety and child protection measures are being fully complied with, as well as the Free school's own plan as set out in its application. This should extend to the right to examine all textbooks used by the school. This is not to allow the LEAs to judge the pedagogy being employed but to ensure that no textbook contradicts the requirement that any values being taught respect individual liberty and human rights.

This right to observe could offer benefits in both directions, representing an opportunity for innovative practice to be seen and, if appropriate, replicated in the community schools under LEA control. In this respect, the intention is that local education authorities will take on a new role as education commissioners, assessing and spreading better practices.

Although cases such as this would hopefully be rare, there would need also to be a system in place that would allow any Free school that is failing to fulfil the minimum standards to be shut down. However, it would also be important to protect Free schools from arbitrary closure by political bodies. Otherwise, stability could not be guaranteed and that would impede the long-term planning of these institutions as well as the opportunity for external invest-ment. Therefore, once a school has been established, it should have a right to a judicial appeal against any decision to shut it down, and should be allowed to continue operating until a decision has been reached.

Non-selective and transparent admissions

Free schools should be given as much freedom as is reasonably possible. However, pupil admission is one area in which as much power as possible should be delegated directly to parents. Any Free school, with the exception of schools for pupils with special needs, should be non-selective and be required to accept any pupil that is eligible to receive a mainstream state-funded education in the UK. This should apply strictly during primary and secondary years (up to the age of 16). However, Free schools should be able to set minimum qualifications for admission to their sixth-form courses.

In the event of over-subscription, a Free school will have to accept pupils in the order in which they apply. The only exception to this should be siblings of pupils already attending the independent school, who could be permitted to have priority in the queue for places. If too many parents apply simultaneously, offers of school places should be decided by lottery. There should be no selection through ability banding, academic competition, or by faith. Hence, the admissions system will be as fair, transparent and simple as possible.

Preventing segregation by admissions

As has been shown in Sweden, formal equality of access is not enough in all cases to ensure that every family understands the system and uses it. We can predict with confidence that middle-class families will be the first to make use of the system and this might exacerbate segregation, at least in the short term. So there must, in addition to formal equality in admissions, be some schemes in place specifically designed to ensure that parents who are not normally engaged in the system are able to make an informed choice.

School Choice advisers were another initiative of the Education and Inspections Act 2006.[3] Their designated role is to help parents choose a school suitable for their children and to navigate the admissions process. However, like the Schools Commissioner, they currently exist in a form of stasis, unable to really champion parent choice when it is so limited and apt to be overruled by other selection criteria. With the admissions process simplified and school choice made a reality, their role could focus exclusively on helping less advantaged families make a good choice of school for their children. There is some concern over whether choice advisers can offer advice that is truly independent from their associated local education authority (which may have an interest in directing children to under-subscribed schools). Once genuine choice is available, there would have to be a review to see if this is true and whether the cause is a lack of investment in school choice advice or other structural failings.

In addition to this initiative, all local education authorities (LEAs) should be required to distribute, for every academic year, a brochure, available in all languages appropriate for that locality, describing all schools (state and free) in their area to local families. Free schools should be required to provide the results of their external assessments to the LEA for publication, thus allowing parents to have access to those outcome indicators. This brochure should accompany a simple form by means of which parents can register their children for schools with places available, or add their names to a waiting list for schools that are already full. Although making a choice should not be a statutory requirement for parents, the intention of this scheme would be to ensure that as many parents as possible make an active choice even though many will doubtless continue to choose a local state school. This is the approach that has proved instrumental in improving performance across all schools in the Stockholm district of Nacka. By introducing this in all local authorities from the beginning, it should prevent the problems of segregation, present in some parts of the Swedish school system, from emerging when school choice is established in the UK.

In the long term, complicated selection and admission procedures should be phased out from the rest of the state sector. Comprehensive schools, specialist schools and academies that are currently permitted piecemeal elements of selection should be reformed so that pupils living nearby have priority, and that any excess capacity is offered to parents on a first-come-first-served basis. This would leave grammar schools and existing faith schools as anomalies under a system that is otherwise completely non-selective. Since these school types represent the most successful elements of the current school system, it would be rash to abolish their ability to select until it could be shown that Free schools were as successful at generating better educational outcomes. Currently existing faith schools should not be compelled to opt into being Free schools.

Equitable per-pupil funding

Free schools should be paid for each pupil they accept. This money should be taken from the budget of the local education authority associated with the pupil. This should not be too difficult to build into the current system as most schools in the maintained sector are already paid approximately according to the number of pupils they accept. They should not be permitted to accept top-up fees or make expensive demands on parents, such as by having a particularly costly compulsory school uniform.

The exact amount per pupil will depend on the level of investment currently available to the whole education sector at the time of reform, but perhaps the fairest method of calculating it would be to base it on the national expenditure on each pupil by all local authorities. That way, there would be no funding variation between pupils coming from different local authorities.

On the other hand, it must be acknowledged that local authorities still have the responsibility to provide education for each child in their district. To have all of the average cost of educating a pupil withdrawn from LEAs will impede their ability to guarantee that education. To offset that, it might be prudent to allow LEAs to deduct a 'risk premium' for each pupil that goes to a Free school of perhaps five per cent of total expenditure per pupil. That would mean that the LEA would be able to put money aside or invest in keeping a few additional school places open in local state schools in the case of any pupils choosing to leave an independent school.

Alternatively, the spare capacity could be made more explicit, by allowing some pupils who choose an independent school in any single local authority to have their school places paid for via central government. In other words, local authorities would have their budgets maintained by the Treasury in line with the number of new school places, perhaps up to the first few hundred Free-school pupils. That would certainly create an incentive for local authorities to welcome Free schools, as they would accompany more direct investment. It would be important that there was a strict limit on this investment, however. Otherwise, there would be no financial incentive in place for the local authorities to improve standards in their own state schools.

Local authorities should also be able to raise funds by leasing school premises that they own to Free schools, a common practice in Sweden.

Weighting investment towards the economically disadvantaged

In order to ensure that pupils from poorer backgrounds are among the first pupils to be served by Free schools, there is a case to be made for 'weighting' the per-pupil funding in their favour: a low-income pupil premium. This could be generated using the existing measure that tests pupils' eligibility for free school meals. Some weighting would be necessary anyway in order to ensure that Free schools could afford to pay for the free school meals that, like all other state-funded schools, they would be required to provide. A premium equivalent to 20 per cent of average per pupil funding (including the free school meal allowance) would encourage independent schools to open in poorer areas and market their education to low-income families. From the extra funding, Free schools might choose to invest in some of the 'wrap-around' services, such as breakfast clubs, that the government is currently trying to enforce from above or to attract teachers with more experience and training.

Non-coercive financial incentives along these lines are more likely to encourage direct engagement between schools and parents as no child is being 'deployed' involuntarily into a school. For each family the choice has to be active, meaning that schools will have to be active in attracting them, especially if they want the additional low-income pupil premium.

Greater flexibility for children with special educational needs (SEN)

Additional investment should be made available to children with specific needs. It is also important that any increased diversity offered by Free schools is as accessible as possible to SEN children. Under the current system, some SEN children are assessed by their LEA and issued with a statement detailing their needs. This allows parents to choose which state, special school or independent school they would like their child to attend or what type of education provided outside of school they would like (such as extra tuition).

The law should be changed so that, in addition to the options currently available, the LEA should be required to establish an explicit monetary value for each statement (with a statutory minimum for each SEN set nationally). Parents should have direct control over this money to pay a specialist education provider if that is appropriate. However, Free schools that have 'in-house' facilities for children with a particular SEN that the parents choose should also be permitted to accept the additional money on top of the voucher already available. The result of this would be that parents of SEN children would have the greatest number of options under the reform: state maintained schools, specialist schools, Free schools (specialist or mainstream), independent schools and any education providers outside of school willing to accept the money made available by the LEA. The intention here is to ensure the system is especially adapted and, whenever possible, inclusive of SEN children.

In the longer term, it would be wise to standardise funding arrangements across the entire state sector so that each pupil represents an equivalent level of funding whichever school they choose to attend whether it is state or free. This would mean that no type of school would have a particular advantage over others and all can compete for pupils on an equal footing. This would also provide a suitable mechanism for systematically increasing the funding for pupils in any circumstances that need addressing, including expelled pupils (who currently tend to languish in pupil referral units), the increasing number of children with English as a second language and children with disabilities. The long-term aim has to be to extend the freedom to choose to the whole sector so that no one, whatever their background or needs, is forced to 'make do' with provision that they find inadequate.

No capital grants

The method of funding Free schools should be exclusively based on the per-pupil measure. The purpose of this is to ensure the only funding stream for Free schools is controlled by parent choice. This will create the correct incentives for Free schools to pursue the best interests of pupils as mediated by parents.

There is an argument that a policy that involves allowing new schools to open must set aside funds for initial capital investment (indeed, this is a cornerstone of Labour's academy scheme). The evidence from Sweden, however, suggests that this is unnecessary since schools can find innovative ways of generating initial finance and tend to use rented premises rather than building entirely new schools. The promise of stable funding based on engaging with individual pupils creates the right structure to encourage long-term planning. The risk with making extra funds available from statutory sources is that it misdirects the attention of school managers towards lobbying government for more investment in their school. This would create an incentive to adapt their profile to impress politicians and civil servants, rather than design their school programme with the exclusive purpose of engaging with potential pupils and impressing parents.

Reduce the need for planning permission

A major barrier to new schools being established is the lack of areas on which schools can be situated according to local planning laws. Left unreformed, this will prevent Free schools from opening fast enough to cope with demand for good school places. This limitation is artificial and can be resolved relatively easily. Schools are currently only allowed to be established on areas with land designation that applies narrowly to public buildings in non-commercial use like churches and schools—the planning category known as D1. The law should be changed so that schools can be permitted to open on land with commercial and industrial designations besides their current category. Careful consideration should be made of whether some residential designations would be suitable for schools as well. This would be especially useful for allowing the development of small local primary schools situated within communities. If enacted, this would allow new schools to open without having to apply to the local council for change of use, and would allow schools to make innovative use of any available property.

Faith Free schools must be non-selective

Groups of any faith should be permitted to apply to open Free schools and be given equal consideration in the application process, so long as the values they intend to teach are compatible with democracy, individual liberty and human rights. Those intending to open a faith school should enjoy a reputable status in their faith community as well as in the wider community.

Faith schools opened as Free schools should have the ability to manage the timetable in line with prayers and other communal religious activity. The curriculum, appointment of staff and codes of acceptable behaviour could also reflect the beliefs of the faith community. Faith schools should not, however, have any ability to select pupils on the basis of religious background or observance. This is to prevent selection on faith as a proxy for selection by social background or academic ability.

There is a reasonable argument that faith schools, at least in the UK, require the ability to select in order to create and maintain a suitable ethos. The Swedish case suggests, however, that this is not always necessary so long as there remains the freedom to decide what happens *within* the school. That way, any Free school, faith or not, is challenged to create an ethos with whoever it attracts, rather than by turning pupils away. It is also likely that the current controversy over faith schools in the UK has been created not so much because non-religious families want their children to attend a faith school as such, but rather that faith schools in some areas have a near monopoly on good education. Once the supply of good school places has been expanded, there will be far less clamouring for access to faith schools and the issue of faith school selection, for those that still retain the right to select pupils, will subside.

Safeguarding social cohesion

One of the main purposes of offering greater independence for schools is to ensure that political institutions do not control what is taught in schools, allowing teachers to exercise their professional discretion and parents to choose what is best for their children. There is one area, however, where the state can place a legitimate obligation on schools and that is with regards to preparing their pupils to be citizens of the United Kingdom, capable of integrating into a pluralist society. It should be noted that although this obligation is considered with respect to Free schools, it is by no means always fulfilled in the current state maintained system. The problem of social cohesion is current and controversial because of this.

In the model advocated here, mention has already been made of the positive requirement to teach a high proportion of lessons in English and the negative requirement not to teach any values incompatible with individual liberty and human rights has been articulated. However, these requirements alone are not necessarily sufficient to prepare children for adult citizenship. At the same time, to require Free schools to teach a particular set of values, decided by the state, would be a great threat to their independent ethos.

The least ideologically compromising solution would oblige schools to teach a short course on the simple *facts* of the political and legal institutions of the UK, including rights available under the law, the electoral system, trial by jury, how legislation is passed through the houses of parliament and some historical knowledge of the development of these institutions. The course should also include some knowledge of international institutions such as the European Union. How schools teach this course should be left up to them, including whether it be taught as a separate subject, in history or in another subject. However, all pupils should be required to learn these basic facts and should be tested using a compulsory national assessment. A Free secondary school that regularly failed to impart this knowledge to its pupils would be told to reform its curriculum to include it or face closure (subject to a proper judicial procedure).

Allow for-profit schools to operate

The idea of allowing commercial companies to own and manage state schools is one of the most controversial areas of this policy but the Swedish case suggests they play an important role in the 'eco-system' of a school sector. For-profit schools expand more rapidly to fulfil demand from families and are less likely to have long waiting lists of disappointed pupils as a consequence. They are more likely to find out where families are poorly served and establish schools there. There is the further advantage that, as the potential to make a profit plays a small but significant role in their motivation, they are more likely to adjust their profiles to exactly what the majority of parents and pupils generally want: safe, high-performing, mainstream-oriented schools. They will rarely have an agenda or attempt to focus on a particular community or subset of pupils. As a consequence, they are likely to be at the forefront, not just of improving educational outcomes, but also of desegregation and inclusion. This is not to say that non-profit Free schools will not achieve the same eventually, only that for-profit schools will do it more rapidly due to their particular incentives to improve and expand.

Hence, it would be a great loss to engage in a school choice reform that excluded for-profit companies. Indeed, it would impede the expansion of school choice and make it far less phenomenal than in Sweden. However, if for-profits prove too controversial on political grounds, it is still essential that some of the underlying principles of a regulated market are maintained: entities of civil society such as non-profit companies and charities must have the ability to maintain ownership of Free schools and have final control over their budget and assets. With that in place, some of the long-term planning and design offered by a competitive environment could be created, even if the incentives generated by for-profit companies would not be present.

Independent schools permitted to opt-in

Many fee-paying independent schools achieve excellent educational outcomes and even attract pupils from abroad. Due to these benefits, they should be left alone by any internal reform of the state maintained sector. It is, however, possible that a suitably reformed state maintained sector would attract many pupils from families currently more likely to use independent schools. This would lead to a contraction of the independent sector, and may lead some independent schools to opt into state funding as Free schools and, of course, accept the limitations of not charging and not selecting pupils. If this were to happen naturally, this would be a symptom, rather than a cause, of growing equality in educational opportunities. Therefore, independent schools opting into the state sector should be permitted but not encouraged.

Foreign pupils permitted to pay to join Free schools

Britain is a popular destination for international students attending university courses, and international pupils attending fee-paying independent schools. Free schools should be permitted to take advantage of this opportunity for additional investment. They should be allowed to set aside school places for foreign students, to choose who to admit and to charge fees (this should not affect any of the rules regarding British students). The intention of this is to allow Free schools to benefit in a similar way that British universities do currently, by charging fees to foreign students that reflect the global market value of the education on offer. This would allow schools to develop their facilities even more rapidly than with ordinary per-pupil funding provided to Free schools, to the benefit of the British pupils who attend for free.

A 'goal-based' National Curriculum

Another necessary but long-term approach to improvement is the disengagement of the government from decisions about what is taught in schools and how it is taught. While it is possible to drive up standards in some schools by allowing them to be exempt from some of the strictures of the National Curriculum, that is of little help to the majority of schools that are still heavily regulated and struggle to adapt to pupil needs.

This regulation should be reduced and withdrawn as less coercive means of school improvement, competition and co-operation, are introduced. The government still has a limited role to play in setting some (not all) of the aims of the education sector: some of the content of what children should know and some of the skills they should have. Hence, the National Curriculum should establish goals rather than teaching methods and lesson content. It is worth emphasising that this curriculum should not be so comprehensive that it crowds out discretion within schools, but merely sufficient to ensure that all children have some essential skills and knowledge for adult life. The assumption is that teachers and schools will, whenever possible, push their pupils further than what is required by the state and seek to teach more than the content that can easily be assessed.

Freedom in qualifications and assessments

As described in more detail in chapter two, the government currently maintains a stranglehold over the assessment of pupils through a combination of targets and outright bans on some sorts of qualifications. Free schools and, eventually, all schools in the maintained sector ought to have the freedom to choose what qualifications suit each pupil. That way, there should be a growth in more rigorous assessment for both academic and vocational qualifications. Schools eager to demonstrate the abilities of their pupils rather than to score well according to bureaucratically developed rankings would drop poor quality courses. This may not lead to a proliferation of new qualifications as several alternatives already exist. Fee-paying independent schools increasingly use IGSE courses, for example. The advantage of a more open system would be that schools could select the forms of assessment that help to reflect the genuine abilities and skills that their pupils have, rather than the narrow criteria that many compulsory national examinations rely on at the moment. This would also help the school curriculum to be broadened, as there would be less reliance on the currently limited choice of courses.

Government still has a role in assessment. There is a case for having a small number of compulsory national assessments in key years. The purpose of these would be to offer a comparative measurement of school standards, rather than to offer qualifications to pupils. A central body, such as the Qualifications and Curriculum Authority, could play a useful role in focusing not on regulating qualifications, but comparing them. At the moment, qualifications are given artificial values without actually testing how robust those values are. A far more useful centrally managed project would simply establish the comparative merits of each one in measuring the abilities of pupils using criteria set out by those who actually need to know what qualifications mean (in the main, universities and employers). In that sense, even less mainstream qualifications could be discovered to be worth a certain number of UCAS points (in the case of university admissions) or represent a certain level of expertise in the case of vocational skills.

The end of a centralised system of inspection

Over the long term, LEAs should be permitted to expand their role of commissioning education in community schools and observing local Free schools to inspecting their community schools as well, allowing the centralised system currently provided by Ofsted to be phased out. They should be given greater independence including the power to interpret the National Curriculum and other guidelines for their local context. They should also be permitted to adapt some of the content of the lessons in their community schools and use alternative pedagogies that have been shown to be popular and effective in Free schools. This way, even with a majority of schools still under state ownership, a wide diversity of successful schools that are responsive to local needs could be developed within the state sector.

Conclusion

When school choice is proposed, a common response from government is that families do not really want a choice of schools, but a good local school. This is an accurate statement but, especially considering the evidence presented here, slightly misses the point: a good local school for every child is a desired outcome, but not a solution in itself. On the outcomes, everyone is in agreement. It is the solution that is controversial. However, this school choice proposal merely aims to extend some of the same powers to all that are currently only enjoyed by the middle classes and, in the process, make a good local school for every child a possibility.

Once it has been established that school choice is not an aim in itself but a mechanism to improve educational outcomes, it becomes clear that opposition to it must, on some level, imply a preference for some other mechanism for deciding what happens in schools. This mechanism is not usually articulated. However, if parents are refused a choice of schools, then it is clear that someone else must be taking those decisions instead: Whitehall officials.

The international evidence suggests that schools perform better when given more freedom from government, so it seems that it is indeed teachers and parents that make better choices. The question, therefore, is not really whether school choice will always produce perfect outcomes but whether there is anyone prepared to defend the only available alternative: control by central bureaucracy. Does anyone still believe, knowing what we do now, what Douglas Jay, author of the Socialist Case and member of parliament from 1946 to 1983, once argued: '...in the case of education, the gentleman in Whitehall really does know better what is good for people than the people know themselves.'

Notes

Introduction

1   Mill, J. S., *On Liberty*, New York: bartleby.com, 1999:
    http://www.bartleby.com/130/

2   See: Commanding English – the key to the world:
    http://www.engelska.se./resources/ies/documents/
    IES_brochure.pdf

3   See: Internationella Engelska Skolan
    http://www.engelska.se/?get=content&action=view&id=127-92

4   Mill, *On Liberty*, New York: bartleby.com, 1999.

5   Smithers, A., 'Blair's Education: an international perspective',
    Centre for Education and Employment Research, University of
    Buckingham, 2007: http://www.suttontrust.com/reports/
    SuttonTrust_BlairsEd19June.pdf

1: School Choice in Sweden

1   Hlavac, M., *Open Access for UK Schools*, London: Adam Smith
    Institute, 2007, p. 6.

2   'Proposition om valfrihet och fistaende skolor' (Prop. 1991/92:95),
    referenced in Hlavac, *Open Access for UK Schools*, 2007, p. 5.

3   'Valfrihet i skolan' (Prop.1992/93:230), referenced in Hlavac, *Open
    Access for UK Schools*, 2007, p. 5.

4   Bergström, F. and Blank, M., *A Survey on the Development of
    Independent Schools in Sweden*, London: Reform, 2005.

5   Böhlmark, A. and Lindahl, M., *The Impact of School Choice on Pupil
    Achievement, Segregation and Costs: Swedish Evidence*, The Institute
    for the Study of Labor (IZA), 2007, p. 7:
    ftp://repec.iza.org/RePEc/Discussionpaper/dp2786.pdf

6   Hlavac, *Open Access for UK Schools*, 2007, p. 5.

7   Presentation by Patrik Levin: 'The Swedish School System',
    Skolverket.

8   Official Nacka brochure: 'The Right to Choose School':
    http://www.nacka.se/default/PlatsID.8/vis.1

9   Böhlmark and Lindahl, *The Impact of School Choice on Pupil Achievement, Segregation and Costs: Swedish Evidence'*, 2007, p. 17.

10 Calculated using OECD PPP figures:
    http://www.oecd.org/dataoecd/48/18/18598721.pdf

11 OECD, 'Education at a Glance', 2007:
    http://www.oecd.org/document/30/0,3343,en_2649_39263294_39251
    550_1_1_1_1,00.html

12 Hlavac, *Open Access for UK Schools*, 2007, pp. 6-10.

13 Sandström, M. in Stanfield, J. (ed.), *The Right to Choose? — Yes, Prime Minister!'*, London: Adam Smith Institute, 2006, p. 7.

14 'Social Democrats plan school profits ban', *The Local*, 6 August 2007: http://www.thelocal.se/4529/20060806/

15 Bergström and Blank, *A Survey on the Development of Independent Schools in Sweden*, 2005, p. 10.

16 Bergström and Blank, *A Survey on the Development of Independent Schools in Sweden*, 2005, p. 18.

17 See: Swedish Association of Independent Schools:
    http://www.friskola.se/Om_friskolor_Friskolorna_i_siffror_DXNI-
    25907_.aspx

18 'Village schools "Facing closure"', *BBC News*, 27 January 2008:
    http://news.bbc.co.uk/1/hi/education/7211497.stm

19 Bergström and Blank, *A Survey on the Development of Independent Schools in Sweden*, 2005, p. 15.

20 www.pysslingen.se

21 www.vittra.se

22 Presentation by Patrik Levin: 'The Swedish School System', Skolverket.

23 See: http://www.skolverket.se/sb/d/374/a/1215

24 See: http://www.skolverket.se/sb/d/374/a/1288

25 Lundh, S. and Hwang, S., *School Choice and its Effects In Sweden*, Offprint of Report 230 – Summary, Skolverket (The Swedish National Agency for Education), Stockholm, 2003, p. 7.

26 Lundh and Hwang, *School Choice and its Effects In Sweden*, 2003, p. 8.

27 Skolverket, *Educational Results National Level, Part 1* (report 290), Stockholm, Sweden, 2007, p. 19.

28 Skolverket, *Educational Results National Level, Part 1* (report 290), 2007, p. 59.

29 Lundh and Hwang, *School Choice and its Effects In Sweden*, 2003, p. 7.

30 Sandström, F. M., and Bergström, F., *School Vouchers in Practice: Competition Won't Hurt You!* The Research Institute of Industrial Economics, Working Paper No. 578, Stockholm, Sweden, 2002, p. 6: http://www.civitas.org.uk/pdf/Sandstrom.pdf

31 Sandström and Bergström, *School Vouchers in Practice*, 2002, p. 23.

32 Ahlin, A., *Does School Competition Matter? Effects of a Large-Scale School Choice Reform on Student Performance*, Department of Economics, Uppsala University, Uppsala, Sweden, 2003, pp. 23-24: http://www.nek.uu.se/pdf/wp2003_2.pdf

33 Ahlin, *Does School Competition Matter?*, 2003, p. 21.

34 Ahlin, *Does School Competition Matter?*, 2003, p. 19.

35 Ahlin, *Does School Competition Matter?*, 2003, p. 19.

36 Ahlin, *Does School Competition Matter?*, 2003, p. 19.

37 Böhlmark and Lindahl, *The Impact of School Choice on Pupil Achievement, Segregation and Costs*, 2007, pp. 41-42.

38 Böhlmark and Lindahl, *The Impact of School Choice on Pupil Achievement, Segregation and Costs*, 2007, p. 42.

39 Böhlmark and Lindahl, *The Impact of School Choice on Pupil Achievement, Segregation and Costs*, 2007, p. 42.

40 Böhlmark and Lindahl, *The Impact of School Choice on Pupil Achievement, Segregation and Costs*, 2007, p. 42.

41 http://www.schoolmatters.com/

42 'Social Democrats plan school profits ban', *The Local*, 6 August
    2006: http://www.thelocal.se/4529/20060806/

43 Sandström, in Stanfield, J. (ed.), *The Right to Choose? — Yes, Prime
    Minister!*, 2006, p. 7.

44 http://www.pearsoned.co.uk/AboutUs/Edexcel/

2: The Challenge for School Reform in England

1   OECD: *PISA 2006: Science Competencies for Tomorrow's World*, 4
    December 2007: http://www.pisa.oecd.org/document/
    2/0,3343,en_32252351_32236191_39718850_1_1_1_1,00.html

2   Twist, L., Schagen, I. and Hodgson, C., *Readers and Reading: the
    National Report for England 2006* (PIRLS: Progress in International
    Reading Literacy Study), National Foundation for Educational
    Research, Slough, 2007: http://www.nfer.ac.uk/ publications/
    pdfs/downloadable/PIRLSreport.pdf

3   Twist, Schagen and Hodgson, *Readers and Reading*, 2007, p. 90.

4   Brooks, G., *Trends in standards of literacy in the United Kingdom, 1948-
    1996*, National Foundation for Educational Research, Slough, 1997:
    http://www.leeds.ac.uk/educol/documents/000000650.htm

5   Paton, G., 'Failure to teach three Rs "damaging economy"',
    Telegraph, 19 January 2008:
    http://www.telegraph.co.uk/news/main.jhtml;jsessionid=LKNHRC
    RV4RG33QFIQMGCFFOAVCBQUIV0?xml=/news/2008/01/18/nthr
    eers118.xml

6   de Waal, A. and Cowen, N., *Ready to Read?*, London: Civitas, 2007:
    http://www.civitas.org.uk/pdf/readytoread.pdf

7   Blanden, J. and Machin S., 'Recent Changes in Intergenerational
    Mobility in the UK: A Summary of Findings', London: Sutton
    Trust, 2007:http://www.suttontrust.com/reports/Summary.pdf

8   'University participation "virtually unchanged" for working
    classes', London: Institute of Education, 29 January 2008:
    http://ioewebserver.ioe.ac.uk/ioe/cms/get.asp?cid=1397&1397_1=18
    010

9   DCSF: National Curriculum Assessment, GCSE and Equivalent
    Attainment and Post-16 Attainment by Pupil Characteristics in
    England, 2006/07, 27 November 2007, table 8:
    http://www.dcsf.gov.uk/rsgateway/DB/SFR/s000759/SFR38-
    2007.pdf

10 UNICEF, Child poverty in perspective: An overview of child well-
    being in rich countries, *Innocenti Report Card* 7, UNICEF Innocenti
    Research Centre, Florence, 2007. http://www.unicef-
    icdc.org/presscentre/presskit/reportcard7/rc7_eng.pdf

11 Compiled by Reform:
    http://www.reform.co.uk/website/education/schoolssystemperform
    ance/funding.aspx

12 Based on press releases published in January 2008 by the DCSF:
    http://www.dfes.gov.uk/pns/newslist.cgi

13 Based on figures from the Economic Research Council's database of
    quangos: http://quangos.ercouncil.org/stats/

14 Department for Education and Skills, 'First Release GCSE and
    equivalent examination results in England 2005/06 (revised)',
    London, 10 January 2007: http://www.dfes.gov.uk/rsgateway/
    DB/SFR/s000702/SFR01-2007V1.pdf

15 'Top grade for 24.1 per cent of A-levels', *BBC News*, 17 August
    2006: http://news.bbc.co.uk/1/hi/education/4801035.stm

16 Coe, R., 'Changes in standards at GCSE and A-level: Evidence from
    ALIS and YELLIS', CEM centre, Durham University, 2007:
    http://www.cemcentre.org/documents/CEM%20Extra/Specia
    lInterests/Exams/ONS%20report%20on%20changes%20at%2
    0GCSE%20&%20A-level.pdf

17 Coe, R., 'Changes in standards at GCSE and A-level: Evidence from
    ALIS and YELLIS', CEM centre, Durham University, 2007.

18 Smithers, A., 'Do School Exams Need Reforming?', Centre for
    Education and Employment Research, University of Buckingham,
    2005.

19 'Are the league tables "absurd"?', *BBC News*, 13 January 2005:
    http://news.bbc.co.uk/1/hi/education/4172749.stm

20 DCSF: GCE/VCE A/AS and Equivalent Examination Results in England, 2006/07, Table 11: http://www.dfes.gov.uk/rsgateway/DB/SFR/s000769/index.shtml

21 'Call to consider "easy A-levels"', *BBC News*, 4 September 2004: http://news.bbc.co.uk/1/hi/england/wear/3626496.stm; full figures for variations between subjects up to 2006 are available at http://www.alisproject.org/RenderPage.asp?LinkID=11625001

22 'Freshers: school didn't help me make the right choice', Association of Colleges, 29 September 2006, London: http://www.aoc.co.uk/en/newsroom/aoc_news_releases.cfm/id/C45 CD64E-8328-498B-9B6A7D224EBD918B/page/9

23 Royal Society of Chemistry, 'Chinese maths level embarrasses English system', 27 April 2007, London: http://www.rsc.org/AboutUs/News/PressReleases/2007/ChineseMaths.asp

24 Curtis, P., 'A-level pupils urged to spurn "soft" subjects', *Guardian,* 12 August 2005: http://education.guardian.co.uk/alevels/story/0,,1548150,00.html

25 'IOP Chief on A-level results', London: Institute of Physics, 18 August 2005: http://www.iop.org/News/Community_News_Archive/2005/news_5771.html

26 Lipsett, A., 'History A-level under threat, says exams head', *Guardian*, 6 August 2007: http://education.guardian.co.uk/schools/story/0,,2142843,00.html

27 Tough S. and Brooks, R, 'School Admissions: Fair choice for parents and pupils', London: Institute for Public Policy Research, June 2007, p. 9: http://www.ippr.org/publicationsandreports/publication.asp?id=546

28 DfES, School Admissions Code, 2007: http://www.dfes.gov.uk/sacode

29 DFSC: 'Schools and Local Authorities told to comply with school admissions law', 17 January 2008: http://www.dfes.gov.uk/pns/DisplayPN.cgi?pn_id=2008_0013

30 Paton, G., 'Education gap has widened under Labour', *Telegraph*, 29 January 2008:

http://www.telegraph.co.uk/news/main.jhtml;jsessionid=NLPXZ5B
JXPVITQFIQMFSFFWAVCBQ0IV0?xml=/news/2008/01/29/nedu129
.xml

31 Paton, G., 'Top schools should allocate places "by lottery"',
   Telegraph, 17 January 2008:
   http://www.telegraph.co.uk/news/main.jhtml?xml=/news/2008/01/1
   7/nschool117.xml

32 See Independent Schools Council Census data:
   http://www.isc.co.uk/FactsFigures_PupilNumbers.htm

33 See Independent Schools Council Census data:
   http://www.isc.co.uk/FactsFigures_GCSEResults.htm

34 See Independent Schools Council Census data:
   http://www.isc.co.uk/FactsFigures_ALevelResults.htm

35 Smithers, A., 'Blair's Education: an international perspective',
   Centre for Education and Employment Research, University of
   Buckingham, 2007: http://www.suttontrust.com/reports/
   SuttonTrust_BlairsEd19June.pdf

36 'Mori Omnibus Wave 16 Parents Survey 2004', Ipsos Mori, 11 May
   2004.

37 Ireson, J. and Rushforth, K., 'Mapping and Evaluating Shadow
   Education', Institute of Education, University of London, 2005.

38 Curtis, P., 'Grammar schools fuelling segregation, academics find',
   Guardian, 1 February 2008: http://education.guardian.co.uk/
   specialreports/grammarschools/story/0,,2250452,00.html

39 Katwala, S., 'Breaking the cycle of disadvantage', Fabian Society, 11
   December 2007: http://fabians.org.uk/events/katwala-life-chances-
   07/speech

40 Charity Commission: Charities and Public Benefit, January 2008:
   http://www.charity-commission.gov.uk/publicbenefit/
   publicbenefit.asp

41 Smithers, 'Blair's Education: an international perspective', 2007.

42 Smithers, 'Blair's Education: an international perspective', 2007.

43 For a full discussion, see Whelan, R. (ed.), *The Corruption of the Curriculum*, London: Civitas, 2007.

44 For a full discussion, see de Waal, A., *Inspection, Inspection, Inspection!*, London: Civitas, 2006.

45 Frean, A., 'Grammars 'should be forced to abandon selection', *The Times*, 1 February 2008: http://www.timesonline.co.uk/ tol/life_and_style/education/article3285511.ece

46 Tough and Brooks, 'School admissions: Fair choice for parents and pupils', 2007, p. 10.

47 Smithers, 'Blair's Education: an international perspective', 2007.

3: A School Choice Policy for England

1 http://www.dfes.gov.uk/schoolscommissioner/

2 For a wider discussion see: http://www.civitas.org.uk/ pdf/CowenSchoolChoiceJan2007.pdf

3 http://choiceadvice.dfes.gov.uk/dfes2/modules.php?name=Home